Planting Your Purpose

PLANTING

Your

PURPOSE

A 20 Day Guide to
Discovering God's Calling

ALEC KASSAN

PLANTING YOUR PURPOSE

A 20 Day Guide to Discovering God's Calling

ISBN   978-1-5445-0926-6 *Hardcover*

978-1-5445-0925-9 *Paperback*

TO THOSE WHO ARE CALLED

AND THOSE WHO ARE CRITICIZED.

CONTENTS

The members of the council were amazed when they saw the boldness of Peter and John, for they could see that they were ordinary men with no special training in the Scriptures. They also recognized them as men who had been with Jesus.

—ACTS 4:13 NLT

Amos replied, "I'm not a professional prophet, and I was never trained to be one. I'm just a shepherd, and I take care of sycamore-fig trees. But the LORD called me away from my flock and told me, 'Go and prophesy to my people in Israel.'"

—AMOS 7:14–15 NLT

It's not important who does the planting, or who does the watering. What's important is that God makes the seed grow. The one who plants and the one who waters work together with the same purpose. And both will be rewarded for their own hard work. For we are both God's workers. And you are God's field. You are God's building.

—1 CORINTHIANS 3:7–9 NLT

VISIT

www.PlantingYourPurpose.com

FREE BONUS

RESOURCES

SCAN ME

20% Off
PLANTING YOUR
PURPOSE

Downloadable
Worksheets
& Videos

INTRODUCTION

Where there is no vision, the people perish.

—PROVERBS 29:18 KJV

It doesn't matter how fast you can go; it doesn't matter how much passion you have, and it doesn't matter how much energy you put into something. If you don't have a vision and clarity on the destination you want to reach, you'll simply never get there.

—DEAN GRAZIOSI

I want to thank you for taking the initiative that not many people make. When it comes to finding purpose and fulfillment, a lot of people settle for less or avoid their calling in life.

And when it comes to finding one's calling or pursuing more fulfillment, we are often met with the popular suggestions to...

"Just do what you're good at," or "Do what you're passionate about."

Although this advice may sound good, there's not much substance in terms of how to act on it. Plus, we've all had jobs or pursued projects in the past where we did the things we loved but still found ourselves unfulfilled or feeling as though God was calling us toward something greater.

Can you recall what your first job was?

For some of you, getting that first job was probably an exciting time because you saw the work as a stepping-stone toward greater opportunities. For others, you may have taken the job simply out of necessity. Either way, I'm sure you took the job based on what the job could provide for you, and I'm also sure you aren't still working there.

Maybe you left because there was a better gig. Maybe you stopped working there because it wasn't paying enough. Or maybe you quit because it was a toxic work environment. But imagine if you still worked at that first job. Imagine the unfulfillment and passionless life you would have been living if you still worked there.

Now imagine if you went the rest of your life still working at that same job.

Doesn't sound very pleasant or fulfilling, does it? In fact, I'm sure you feel like you'd be wasting your life if you did that.

The first job I ever worked wasn't anywhere close to feeling fulfilling. During my sophomore year in high school, I applied to work in one of those stereotypical busboy jobs at a local Italian restaurant.

Growing up in church, I learned to find satisfaction in serving others. So being able to serve *and* get paid for it was truly amazing at the time.

My friend Evan, who was also a sophomore, had reassured me that being a busboy with him would be good. Evan was confident that us working together would be constant fun.

He told me about all the money he was making, saying how the extra cash gave him so much freedom! He could buy his own video games and order his own food, all without needing to ask, or beg, for his parents' permission. But the thing that convinced me to take the job was the amazing leftover food. After the restaurant closed, we got to take home all the prepared food that wasn't served.

The typical work schedule entailed leaving school at 2:30 p.m. sharp, getting to the neighboring town's upscale Italian restaurant at 3 p.m., and working till about 2 a.m. The pay was okay, but the tips were fantastic, and the free food was delicious!

However, the long hours and late nights soon got to me. The work was constant, my back was aching, and the pay started to not seem worth the time and energy. I barely saw my friend Evan since we were continuously running around the restaurant. My motivation to stay faded rapidly.

When I made up my mind to quit, I walked into the kitchen, went to the manager, and put in my two weeks' notice. His response was rather shocking.

In his thick Italian accent, he emphatically exclaimed, "What is dis two-week notice? You work, you stay, you quit, you leave!"

The kitchen went silent. I was at a loss of words.

All the staff froze and stared at the manager and me. I tried explaining that I would be willing to work until I could be replaced, but I was quickly met again with the sharp reply, "No, no, no. You work, you stay, you quit, you leave."

So I left. I lasted three months at that job.

How is it that we can start something feeling very zealous, but end up falling out of love with what we are doing?

Maybe you've struggled with a sense of purpose or fulfillment too. When there are many possibilities ahead of you, sometimes it's hard to know the best way to go. It seems that any option is a good option. But deep down, we all want to know, which option is best?

When I quit working as a busboy, I felt a strange shift in my spirit, as though my character was being challenged or my identity was being tested. At that point in my high school career, I had grown to see myself as the type of person who doesn't quit when times get tough.

During the summer prior to taking the busboy job or even starting high school, I was mistakenly signed up to join the high school football team. My friend Tarek had confused me for one of our other friends, Tom, who had expressed interest in playing. Since Tom and I were both overweight, out of shape, and had the same chubby faces, it made sense why my friend Tarek would have confused us.

Instead of ignoring my friend's plea to join the football team, I reluctantly found myself walking on the field for the first day of practice.

Within the first few minutes, coach Satchell shared some wisdom with us that clearly communicated how serious he was about this sport and our involvement in it. He said, "From this point moving forward I want you all to know, if you show up to practice on time, you're late. If you're early, you're on time. And if you're late, don't even bother showing up!"

This stern and authoritative presence of coach Satchell had alienated many of the other kids, but I found his personality and booming presence to be inspiring.

After the first day of practice, I approached him to let him know I didn't think I belonged and couldn't do well on the team. I had no experience in playing football and wasn't any good at the sport, far from it. Many of the kids were better than me and enjoyed the sport way more than I did, which is probably why they signed up in the first place. In contrast, I had accidentally been signed up, and it wasn't even me who did it!

Satchell pointed out that even though the other kids might enjoy football, many of them will quit. For them, joining the team might have started with a passion for the sport or a joy in watching it. However, staying on the team, and doing well, would require more than simply liking the sport.

Coach Satchell began to explain...

"The older boys on this team that do well are the ones who see this sport as something beyond just themselves. They aren't here to simply rack up points on a scoreboard or have a good time. They are here because their identity is in how they perform.

"These boys are trying to become better athletes, which means they are working to grow physically and mentally in order to step into that role. They are here because the way they act and overcome challenges on the field is how they'll learn how to act and overcome challenges in the real world.

"If you don't want to be a better football player, then fine. However, that doesn't mean you can't find a greater purpose for being here."

This short talk had me reconsider my decision to leave the team. I thought that by not being super passionate about this sport, I wouldn't benefit from playing it, and the team wouldn't benefit from me being there. Yet from Satchell's experience, he explained that the students who had a higher purpose for playing were the ones that could endure the hardest challenges, have the greatest growth, and bring the most value to the team.

After our talk, I could see that Coach Satchell started to train me in a slightly different way than the rest of the teammates. He wasn't being easier on me. If anything, he knew exactly how to challenge me to my breaking points in every practice.

The way that Satchell trained me differently was by identifying and coaching me toward a higher purpose. He could see that my chubby, soft outside reflected how I felt on the inside. What I wanted was to walk with the same authority and confidence that he had, along with the other influential men in my life. Satchell knew that appealing to the nobler purpose of becoming a stronger and more committed man would be the driving force to help me persevere through practice.

From that point on, I would be on that field at 6:30 a.m. six days a week for my freshman, sophomore, and senior years of high school.

How is it that I could endure three years playing a sport that I did not like, did not get paid for, and wasn't good at...but couldn't endure three months in a job that was air-conditioned, paid well, and wasn't nearly as physically taxing?

Only when I look back can I say that purpose and calling were a key factor as to why I was able to stay on the team, and other kids couldn't. It's also why I couldn't last as a busboy for three months but could be out in the blazing sun and frigid winters just to get tackled.

I believe it is having a purpose, a sense of calling, that allows one to endure. There was a clear vision as to why I was on that football field. It was so I could no longer be a sappy boy and could instead become a strong and unrelenting young man.

The mission, the way in which I would reach the vision, was through experiencing two-a-day practices, showing up every day, and leaving any excuses I had off the field, which is quite contradictory to the common career advice we hear: "Do what you're good at or passionate about."

Calling and purpose are not things that require a dramatic epiphany moment. They don't come from living in the woods or going up to an isolated mountain top. They aren't some singular magical moment where God parts the clouds and clearly writes everything out in the sky.

Many believe that pursuing God's calling in our life consists of doing one predestined holy task for the rest of our life, and if we don't find that one thing, then we're missing out.

But that belief is not true.

God's spirit is pulling us toward something greater than where we are now. Our call is more than just showing up to church on Sunday, and as followers of Jesus, we should desire to do more with our lives than just survive. Like the Israelites in Egypt, we are outgrowing our current situation and need to venture into the desert toward the Promised Land.

Following God's calling in our life is simply the willingness to take one step in the direction where God is pointing and having faith that God will guide you the rest of the way, every step of the way.

WHAT TO EXPECT
ON THIS JOURNEY

We mostly spend [our] lives conjugating three verbs: to Want, to Have, and to Do... forgetting that none of these verbs have any ultimate significance, except so far as they are transcended by and included in, the fundamental verb, to Be.

—EVELYN UNDERHILL

There is a popular culture that is driven by the idea that we need to "have" in order to "get."

We need to HAVE a certain look in order to GET the man or woman of our dreams.

We need to HAVE the newest phone in order to GET the latest features that make life easier.

We need to HAVE a lot of money in order to GET that sense of contentment and peace in our life.

Essentially, we have been led to believe that FILLING our lives can bring about a FULFILLED life.

But very rarely are we encouraged and properly guided in simply BEING. It reminds me of a phrase that goes, "We aren't human gettings; we are human beings."

Humans are one of the only living creatures on earth that struggle with knowing what we were designed for. This has led to a lot, if not all, of the chaos in our lives.

Adam and Eve struggled with their identity of being made in the image of God. As a result, they forgot who they were and ate from the tree of The Knowledge of Good and Evil so that they could be like God and gain more wisdom.

Ironically, they were already made in God's image and could have had wisdom if they had just continued to trust in God. But they stepped away from who they were made to be.

By *being* the person God made you to be, God will *produce* in you the things you need in life.

Yet being the person God made you to be is much easier said than done. When it comes to discovering why something is made, the best way to find out is by either:

1. Asking the creator why it was made

2. Seeing what the thing produces

There are many resources that try and address one's calling by answering why God made mankind. They seek out answers from life's creator, and it seems very fitting in the Christian community to resort to such a viewpoint.

However, this tactic doesn't address the deeper issue of calling; it only focuses on function. For example, if you were to ask the inventor of the hammer, "Why was the hammer made?" they might say, "To drive down or rip up nails," as well as many other things. But the purpose of that hammer varies from user to user. One person may use the hammer to rip down, while the other may use it to build up. Sure, its function is utilized in both scenarios, but its purpose is not defined simply by its function until we see what someone produces with it.

This method of discovering what something is to be by seeing what it produces is best observed when examining plants. A fig tree, despite sharing a variety of the same benefits that other trees offer, such as shade and wood, is known for the types of fruit it produces. The fig tree's unique distinguishing feature is that it produces figs. One could argue that the fig tree's specific calling and purpose is to produce figs.

As Christians, you and I may offer a variety of the same benefits that other people on this earth can provide, but our unique calling is to produce something different.

Your life, like a garden, holds potential to be used by God. He wants to plant seeds in your heart that will produce a fruitful life. What God produces through you is your purpose and calling. It is who God made you to be.

But many of us have struggled to see or maintain the things God has produced in our lives because our gardens are hardened, contaminated, or polluted by the views and values of this world.

If we are to understand our calling and prepare our hearts to produce our purpose, we need to go through the same process that we would for preparing land to produce a fruitful garden. By preparing a fertile heart, Jesus's values can take root and produce purpose in our lives.

Planting Your Purpose will take you through that process.

The various lessons and information in this book were extracted and assembled in order to provide you with a condensed and coherent framework that will guide you on your journey to discover God's calling. Thousands of pages of literature were read so that you will have the most useful strategies, tools, tips, and insights that you can apply in your life immediately. This guide is an attempt to compile all the best wisdom found from dozens of the finest pastors, coaches, psychologists, entrepreneurs, and teachers for how to discover your calling.

Each day, you'll read a section of this book in sequential order (Day 1, Day 2, Day 3, etc.). You are welcome to take notes during each day and write down any thoughts or prayers that come to mind.

There are, however, specific parts of the book that will prompt you to write notes. You MUST take the time to read through and answer the questions in order to get the most out of this book. Passively reading might help to provide you with intellectual knowledge, but change comes from being active in the reading by following the prompts. Therefore, follow the prompts. Write down answers. Take notes and underline, highlight, or circle in the book when you feel it is necessary.

Imperfect notes and imperfect answers are better than no notes or no answers.

As you read through this book, you will also notice blank pages strategically placed throughout. These pages will prompt you to fold the page several times. By doing this, you are creating an internal bookmark. The purpose of these internal bookmarks is to make it easier for you to navigate back to your notes.

For example, in chapter 5, you will be asked to reflect on previous notes. These internal bookmarks will make it easier for you to flip back to those notes.

Each chapter will have a general theme that aids in turning your heart into a fruitful garden.

Chapter 1 is all about laying the "Groundwork," preparing you with the information you need before you can start. It will be full of background information and questions to prepare you for the coming chapters. Think of it as the warmup where you are making sure you have all the tools you need before you get into the field to start gardening.

Chapter 2 will focus on "Cultivating" the heart. Cultivating our heart aids in identifying and removing the surface-level desires that don't allow for true fruitfulness and fulfillment. Proper cultivation is the first step to allowing God to produce in us a fruitful life that is well defined by vision, mission, and purpose. If God's word can't take root in our lives, then we will miss out on experiencing the abundance that can come from planting what few things God has given us.

Chapter 3 takes things deeper as we work on "Digging" out false beliefs and values. Below the surface, there are often deeply buried barriers that are obstructing our development. These deeply buried barriers are often false values or beliefs that, if not addressed, will hinder the depth that God is able to grow us.

Chapter 4 is all about stepping back and "Envisioning" the big picture. What's the endgame? By visualizing the endgame and reflecting on what drives us, we start to imagine what a fruitful life could consist of. If we know what our garden will look like, we can better discern if where we're going is in the right direction.

Chapter 5 is where we finally start "Planting." We'll discover which of Jesus's values deeply penetrate our hearts the most, then use those values—and everything we've learned prior—to craft an empowering and impactful vision and mission that can develop and guide you in being the person God is calling you to be.

Chapter 6 is about "Watering, Grooming, and Weeding" your garden, which are proactive actions. Just like any garden, you don't just plant and leave. You need to manage the ground and care for the plants that you intend to grow. This chapter will help to ensure that you are able to follow through with maintaining your garden and produce the most fruit from it.

Chapter 7 is where we wrap up by "Comparing Baseline Measurements" that were gathered from chapter 1. You'll be able to look back at where you were when you started, and gain confidence from seeing all the progress that has been made.

* * *

This book will show you how to discover who God is leading you to be (the vision) and will point you toward the path that will bring you there (the mission).

Joseph, Moses, and Jesus are fantastic biblical examples of what it looks like to have clarity of vision and mission. They knew their calling and moved with purpose. They were formed by God to fulfill the responsibilities given to them.

We see from Joseph's journey in Genesis how God gave Joseph a vision and then allowed him to go through struggles that not only put his values, integrity, and faith to the test but also put him in the right circumstances that led to him becoming the second-most influential and powerful person in Egypt.

Moses was insecure about speaking to Pharaoh. But through trusting in God and stepping out in faith despite his fears, Moses eventually gained the confidence to face Pharaoh. Moses was able to clearly communicate the vision and mission God placed on his heart, thus leading to the Israelites being set free from Egypt's rule.

But when it comes to having the most successful ministry and widely adopted vision in the Bible, Jesus of Nazareth takes the cake. He had a vision for the renewal of all the world and was on a mission to accomplish that. Billions of people have bought in to it and continue to do so today.

Jesus's ministry, although multifaceted, had a clear goal with a simple vision and mission. Jesus's calling was to serve, seek, and save...

For even the Son of Man did not come to be served, but to serve, and to give his life as a ransom for many.

—MARK 10:45; MATTHEW 20:28 NIV

It is not the healthy who need a doctor, but the sick. I have not come to call the righteous, but sinners.

—MARK 2:17 NIV

For the Son of Man came to seek and to save the lost.

—LUKE 19:10 NIV

Jesus's entire ministry, his calling, the vision, and mission are easily embodied in those single sentences. During the times when things got complicated or things got difficult, or when the people he was trying to serve and save were actively persecuting him, Jesus was capable of viewing it all in the greater perspective of his purpose. When he was up on the cross praying to God, Jesus did not condemn. Rather, he asked for forgiveness on behalf of the sinner.

Then Jesus said, "Father, forgive them, for they do not know what they are doing..."

—LUKE 23:34 NIV

Your calling will be the specifics of the *vision* and *mission* that you'll discover in this guide, and your *purpose* will be the things that are produced from living it out.

The goal isn't to simply talk about the topic of vision and mission in the traditional business sense.

The way we are defining *vision* in this book, is...

> To have clearly defined the roles in one's life,

And the way we are defining *mission* in this book, is...

> The process God will use to shape you into successfully fulfilling that role.

Don't expect this book, or your vision and mission, to provide you all the right answers in every season of life. What you should expect is to have a firmer understanding of the unique combination of biblical values you identify with and the calling God has for you.

This journey will bring you closer to God and feel his love in new ways. If you want to get the most out of this book and experience true transformation, then you *need* to be close to God throughout the whole process.

Trust in the lord with all your heart; do not depend on your own understanding. Seek his will in all you do, and he will show you which path to take.

—PROVERBS 3:5–6

At this point, I'm sure some questions have been answered, while new ones have begun to sprout up. Don't worry. As you get further on this journey, those questions will soon be answered as your calling becomes clearer.

Chapter 1

GROUNDWORK

DAY 1: THE NEED FOR VISION AND MISSION

Christians are tuned in to the idea of calling, and many feel their current jobs are well matched with what they perceive as their calling. But there are also warning signs all around our workplaces. We see some gaps between generations at work and a potential lack of vision for how generations can mentor and support each other. Churches could do a much better job of helping Christians understand how to live out their faith in the workplace—particularly among those who have yet to discover their vocation or integrate faith and work.

—DAVID KINNAMAN AND BILL DENZEL

Many people find their identity and their purpose in the work that they do. Statistically, we will spend about a third of our entire life working. So it makes sense that we might link our identity in the work that we do. For some, they take pride in the job that they get to contribute to. But for many, this isn't the same case.

If you've ever worked at a new job, started a project, or pursued an idea and found yourself losing the fire and satisfaction you had when you first started, you're not alone.

Two thirds of all working millennial and Gen X Christians are dissatisfied with their current roles at work, and 60 percent of millennials and 65 percent of Gen Xers are not fulfilled with the future opportunities that their work offers.[1]

There is a growing desire and a need to find fulfillment.

Many are seeking out guidance and answers. Unfortunately, half of all working Christians feel the church could be doing a better job at helping them understand how to live by faith outside of simply volunteering during Sunday morning services.

Barna Group, a leading research and resource organization focused on analyzing the intersection of faith and culture, conducted a study on how employed Christians understand and value their vocation. Their findings were rather surprising.

Let's imagine your church is starting up a ministry that is made up of a team of five volunteers, all in their twenties.

Statistically, two out of the five people on the team don't know their talents or understand their purpose/calling in ministry. And

---

1   Barna Research, "Millennials Bring Ambition and Optimism to Their Work," Barna Research, May 14, 2019. https://www.barna.com/research/millennials-ambition-optimism-work/.

depending on the demographic, that number could be higher! Fifty-eight percent of millennials, 64 percent of Gen X, and 59 percent of baby boomers don't feel they are aware of the purpose or talents that God has given them.

Michael, one of the volunteers, is a twenty-five-year-old college graduate. Before attending college, Michael read some articles about graduating students who were in debt and unable to find work. It worried him. So he pursued a degree in a field that could both guarantee him a secure job and paid very well. But upon graduating, he found that the secure job he had wasn't providing the fulfillment he desired. Following all the various trends and mainstream advice for finding fulfillment eventually led him to feeling empty and on the wrong path. He wanted to do more with his life and was eager to start by volunteering at his local church. What Michael is portraying are signs of not "Cultivating" the heart (chapter 2). Like soil that becomes hard by being watered too little and by being in the blazing sun for too long, Michael's heart was in the values and belief systems of society for too long without being refreshed by God's spirit. When soil is hard, it is unable to receive the seeds that are planted. On the surface, Michael had become hard and unable to receive what God wanted to give him.

Amanda, another one of the volunteers, is the oldest one on the team at twenty-nine years old. Amanda feels she has her whole life ahead of her! She works at a steady job that she enjoys and makes time to volunteer at church regularly. She has a slight sense that God might want her to start a nonprofit or an organization that can aid the needy. However, Amanda is too focused on other activities and doesn't find the time to think that far into the future.

Amanda sets goals and pursues things that sound exciting and impactful but quickly finds herself taking on any new activity that might pique her interest. Even though her schedule is typically filled with activities from church and work, she wrestles with the feeling that she could be doing more with her life. What Amanda is dealing with are the negative side effects of not "Envisioning" the endgame (chapter 4). Like a gardener looking out at their freshly cleared and cultivated garden, Amanda can see her life has the potential to produce a lot of fruitful work. But to have a productive garden, the gardener first needs to view the land, imagine how the land should be used, and then map out how to use it. Amanda knows she can do great things but lacks the understanding to first imagine where God is ultimately leading her.

Michael and Amanda are certainly enthusiastic about helping. They are both eager to be used in God's kingdom and volunteer, take on projects, or say yes to responsibilities in work and church. Although they may seem keen to be on the team, it is merely an expression of their eagerness to find purpose. They say yes to various projects but not because it is part of their calling. Rather, it is because these work opportunities inspire hope that they might *find* their calling. When that calling isn't found, their enthusiasm will fade and so too will their involvement in the team or project.

Michael and Amanda, despite not having the same struggles, ultimately share the same problem: a lack of vision.

Whether it is a team, an individual, or our self that lacks vision, an absence of focus and understanding of the goal can easily become the sole hindrance to achieving said goal.

However, not every working Christian struggles with having vision or purpose. In fact, three out of five working Christians feel they have a good understanding of their purpose and talents. But there's more to the story than just that.

Even though there may be three on the team who *do* have vision and purpose, two of those three people don't feel that they can utilize their talents or live out their vision and purpose in their vocation.

Jessica, another member on the team, is twenty-three years old and a student at the local college. She's been involved in the church since she was a child, had a phase in high school and college where she wasn't attending consistently, but is now back and more consistent and active in the church than ever before! She is confident in her ability to help wherever she can. Somewhat a jack of all trades, Jessica can write, perform, brainstorm ideas, work with her hands, and manage small teams on short-term tasks. Deep down, she wants to serve and love like Jesus, but she also fears that she might look like a show-off or like she is being picky if she only works in areas where her talents and purpose can best be expressed. Anytime an opportunity comes up that sparks a sense of excitement and joy in her, she worries that it might be a path that would lead her away from God's real calling. Jessica is dealing with deeply buried false beliefs. By not "Digging" deep (chapter 3) to remove these false beliefs, they become barriers that prevent deeper growth and greater fulfillment in her life. The roots of whatever good thing is trying to develop in her life hit these buried barriers, and it leads to behavior of self-sabotage and/or avoidance of one's true calling.

Daniel, on the other hand, wants to be recognized for his successes and dives headfirst into projects. Being the youngest one in the group, recently turning twenty-two, he feels that he needs to be more vocal and energetic in order to be recognized. In church, Daniel wants to use his talents and skills to grow the church. He doesn't just *think* he can contribute a lot of value; he *knows* he can. But due to his lack of experience and self-awareness, his values aren't clearly recognized, and it often feels like Daniel is driven by selfish motives, thus making it hard for others to trust if his heart is in the right place. He genuinely does want to contribute to the growth of God's kingdom and the local church, but Daniel doesn't feel he is being fully utilized and recognized. Daniel's struggle comes from not knowing what values he should be "Planting" (chapter 5). Although a garden may appear to be the most optimal place to plant seeds, not every seed can be planted into every garden. For example, ground that is too wet might kill one type of seed, while another seed can thrive in very wet soil. God knows what values deeply penetrate our hearts. God also knows which values are the most fruitful in our lives. By not knowing the proper values to plant, Daniel is diligent but could be working smarter rather than working harder.

Jessica and Daniel feel that they are unable to live out their calling in the work that they are currently doing. Although they have vision, which is an understanding of the end goal, they are unable to live out their mission, which is the means by which they get to the goal.

Having vision but not being able to live out one's mission will create a perspective that views current jobs or projects merely as stepping-stones. When an opportunity arises that better satisfies an urge to use one's talents, those unable to live by mission start drifting away from previous commitments in order to take on new ones.

What's tragic about not being able to live out one's mission, is that there is a lot of missed potential for the organization, the team, and the individual. It would be like driving a car and never being able to shift it out of first gear. The car has the potential to go faster but never does. If it is you who has vision but can't live it out, then you will never feel fulfilled in any project or job you do and, therefore, will find it hard to commit to any single job or ministry.

But let's say you are the one person on the team who has vision and purpose and feels that their work allows them to step into their calling.

Matthew, the team lead of the program, is twenty-eight years old and a graduate from the best local seminary college. He has a strong awareness of what his purpose is in the church and feels he can fully utilize his God-given talents. Having grown up in church, and been around a community of faithful, well-educated Christians, Matthew had a solid foundation of biblical knowledge. By taking on ambitious projects that are outside his comfort zone, he has been able to mature greatly in faith and character, proving he understands his values, and knows how to leverage his talents/abilities in order to grow a ministry. However, Matthew is prone to overcommitting and taking on too many tasks at once. Matthew finds that anxiety and burnout hold him back from getting the most out of the work he is doing. The problem that Matthew is dealing with comes from not properly "Watering, Grooming, and Weeding" (chapter 6). Like a garden, when we plant seeds, we must meticulously water them. Then when there is growth, we need to groom the branches in order to have the plant produce greater fruit. Finally, we must make sure to constantly weed and remove pests, or else they will crowd out the good things we have planted. Although Matthew has seen growth in his life, without intentionally investing in the few things he has planted and without cutting down or preventing new things from sprouting up, Matthew has encountered diminished growth and unnecessary stresses.

But Matthew reasons with himself that, this time, it will be different. This time, he has a team of passionate people who desire to do more in their life and in the church. A team that will help carry the weight of this program into a fruitful future! A team comprised of Michael, Amanda, Jessica, Daniel, and himself.

So, in a team of five people, statistically, half of the people don't know their vision and purpose. And the other half that does have vision and purpose doesn't feel like their work allows them to step into it. Which means, at best, only one person may actually know their purpose and feel like their work utilizes it.

Team of 5 Working Christians

40%
Don't know their talents
—— or ——
Understand their purpose/calling in ministry

20%
Has vision, purpose
—— and ——
Feels that work allows them to step into calling

40%
Has vision, purpose
—— but ——
Can't utilize talents or live out vision and purpose

Whether you're leading a team or are part of a team, those aren't good odds when trying to run an effective and productive ministry.

One-third of all Christians wish they had a clearer understanding of how to define their calling and purpose. And 37 percent of millennials and Gen Xers wish they had a clearer understanding of how they should be using their gifts and talents to serve God.

When pursuing a new job, project, or idea, many of us make the commitment due to the positive euphoric feelings we get when imagining the limitless possibilities, and fulfillment, that would come from making that decision.

Although a job opportunity or project may provide some good knowledge and experience, many leave jobs feeling deflated because their work didn't bring the fulfillment that was hoped for. Thirty-eight percent of all the working adults in the US seldom/never feel energized by their work,[2] and when our energy is low, so, too, is our passion and motivation to stick with what we started.

Fortunately, we don't need to be an expert, professional, wealthy, wise, or elite to do work that we love.

Loving the work that we do is something we need. Not because getting payed for doing what we love is ideal. Rather, it is because the word of God tells us to do what we love, and love what we do.

If I speak in the tongues of men or of angels, but do not have love, I am only a resounding gong or a clanging cymbal. If I have the gift

2 Barna Research, "Most Pastors Feel Energized and Supported," Barna Research, October 3, 2017. https://www.barna.com/research/most-pastors-feel-energized-and-supported/.

of prophecy and can fathom all mysteries and all knowledge, and if I have a faith that can move mountains, but do not have love, I am nothing. If I give all I possess to the poor and give over my body to hardship that I may boast, but do not have love, I gain nothing... And now these three remain: faith, hope and love. But the greatest of these is love.

—1 CORINTHIANS 13:1–3, 13 NIV

When pursuing our calling, we want to make sure that what we are doing is God's will and not just our own desires. If the work we are doing doesn't line up with the vision God has given us, or if we are hindered in living out the mission, then it becomes very difficult to find and do fulfilling work with love. As followers of Jesus, we want to make sure we are bringing love into every situation. We should have love for the things that we do and the people we help!

By the end of this book, you'll know the values that God wants to have deeply penetrate your heart, inspire you to grow beyond just yourself, and will help you live by the ideals that Jesus teaches.

You'll be able to enter any job or ministry and exemplify Jesus's character and values. You'll know your mission and understand the role and calling that God has planned for you. You'll be moving more confidently and courageously through every door God opens for you while also having the discernment to know which doors should be ignored or left closed.

By the end of this book you'll have:

- An understanding of the good values that'll keep you on the right path

- A knowledge of which biblical values will produce the most fruit in your life

- Defined virtues for maintaining integrity

- A vision that'll give you something to aim for

- A mission for how to get to the vision

- The skills to maximize the fruitfulness in your daily walk with Christ while glorifying God in all areas of your life

To get you warmed up, answer the following questions by writing your response. Just know that there is no right or wrong answer. Simply write whatever you feel is being most honest with yourself in this moment.

- What would your life look like if, for the next month, you made every decision based on the values that Jesus teaches?

- If you were to move confidently and courageously in all areas of your life, what sort of positive ripple effect would you expect to see?

- How would your life feel if you didn't live with purpose? What sort of blessings would you be missing out on? What would a life void of purpose look like?

DAY 2: PURPOSE, VISION, AND MISSION STEMS FROM THE HEART

I will give you a new heart and put a new spirit in you; I will remove from you your heart of stone and give you a heart of flesh.

—EZEKIEL 36:26 NIV

Many have the desire to lead an impactful and meaningful life. This idea of purposeful living is reinforced time and time again through the various businesses, ministries, and individuals who are positively changing the world. They do so according to well-defined, deeply rooted convictions and values. But the sad truth is there are many who go through life aimlessly, who live day to day feeling void of direction, and who can't seem to find purpose.

I want you to know that you have a set of gifts, skills, talents, perspectives, experiences, and passions that are combined in such a unique way that there is literally no one else like you. We have been designed to fulfill unique roles. God places in our hearts a longing to embrace the role that we are made to fill.

Where many go wrong is they approach the world and ask the world what their purpose is. This would be like a seed expecting a gardener to tell it what to grow into.

What needs to be realized is that it is we who are approached by the world and we who are asked what our purpose is. Just how a seed has its function programmed inside its DNA, we have a purpose planted in us by God.

Our meaning and purpose mature from the seeds that God plants in a soft and fertile heart. These seeds, when grown, produce a life that is well defined by vision, mission, and purpose. Therefore, the more we grow, the more that purpose is realized and expressed.

A fruitful life will bring justice where there is injustice, love where there is brokenness, peace where there is strife, resourcefulness where there is poverty, and opportunities where there is oppression.

In order to see and develop purpose, we need a fertile environment for God's truth to take root. And the place where God's truth thrives is in a fertile heart.

All throughout human history, various cultures had conceptions of what the purpose and function of the heart was. Ancient Israelites knew that the heart was an organ inside the chest cavity that kept our body alive. But they also believed the heart was where all our intellectual activity took place. They thought things like decision-making, discernment, and wisdom all came from the heart. They also believed that emotions came from the heart as well.

That is why the Bible emphasizes the importance of knowing the condition of one's heart. If our heart functions to keep us physically alive, mentally sharp, and emotionally stable, then it could be detrimental if our heart is not in the right place. Our decision-making, our discernment, our morals, and our emotions could be leading us down a path of misery and destruction.

Some may argue that circumstances or external factors are what influence people to make evil decisions, but Jesus would argue otherwise.

Anything you eat passes through the stomach and then goes into the sewer. But the words you speak come from the heart—that's what defiles you. For from the heart come evil thoughts, murder, adultery, all sexual immorality, theft, lying, and slander.

—MATTHEW 15:17–19 NLT

What Jesus is saying in this passage is that our words and deeds reflect what is in us. Basically, how we respond to the world reveals who we really are. When we misbehave, get angry, are lazy, say something rude or sarcastic, are mean, or simply say something "we didn't mean," Jesus says that we do these things because these things are within us. A quote that comes to mind that may help to further unpack the passage goes along the lines of...

"Drunk words are sober thoughts."

When people drink too much, alcohol lowers their inhibition, which leads to the person saying or doing things they might not normally do otherwise. For example, people have drunkenly admitted that their past mistakes were more intentional than they originally led others to believe. A lot of times people have drunkenly shared secrets that they had sworn they would never tell. Some have drunkenly confessed sexual desires for someone that they aren't currently in a relationship with. And many have done something like urinate in public when they would normally just use a restroom.

However, the alcohol doesn't *make* a drunk person behave a certain way. The alcohol simply allowed the person to feel confident and comfortable enough to express what was within them this whole time.

Anything you eat passes through the stomach and then goes into the sewer. But the words you speak come from the heart.

—MATTHEW 15:17 NLT

If we ignore behaviors that lead us on a downward spiral toward decay and destruction, it will only spread to other areas of our relationships, ministry, business, and life. It would be like ignoring weeds or not making an effort to remove trash in a garden. The dirt becomes hard, the ground becomes infertile, and plants produce no fruit. Which is why the first exercise we'll go through is simply addressing our current condition in our walk with Jesus. That way, we will see where we need to improve and can measure where the improvement is happening.

BASELINE MEASUREMENTS

So long as we skim across the surface of our lives at high speeds, it is impossible to dig down more deeply.

—JIM LOEHR AND TONY SCHWARTZ, *THE POWER OF FULL ENGAGEMENT*

Having received a bachelor's degree in health and exercise science at Syracuse University, I can say with confidence that baseline measurements are the pivotal beginning to any successful transformation, whether physical or spiritual.

Change and lasting growth is a process that happens slowly at first but grows exponentially over time. Since change feels so slow in the beginning, having a baseline measurement can often be reassuring to the discouraged individual who isn't seeing dramatic change. They can look back at where they were when they started.

They can then gain confidence when they see that progress has been made.

Another benefit is that a baseline measurement shows where we should be keeping our attention. If we know where we should grow and how much we have grown, then we have a greater chance of improving.

Keep in mind, these measurements aren't in a right or wrong answer format. This is to simply track where you are at currently in your journey.

If you are in a challenging season or a fruitful season, keep your response honest and make a side note of any current season you are in.

If you would like a Free PDF Download of this Measurements sheet, head to...

PlantingYourPurpose.com.

In a few words, describe how you are currently doing:

In what ways have you experienced God lately?

List what has been life-giving:

List what has been life-draining:

What things are presently occupying your mind and heart?

From a scale of 1 to 10, 1 being none and 10 being extremely, fill in what you feel for each question.

How excited are you to get to work each morning?

① ② ③ ④ ⑤ ⑥ ⑦ ⑧ ⑨ ⑩

How much do you enjoy what you do for the sake of doing it rather than for what it can provide you?

① ② ③ ④ ⑤ ⑥ ⑦ ⑧ ⑨ ⑩

How accountable do you hold yourself to a set of deeply held values or virtues?

① ② ③ ④ ⑤ ⑥ ⑦ ⑧ ⑨ ⑩

[Greater than 27 means significant sense of purpose]

[Less than 22 means you're going through the motions]

Circle which areas of your life that you would like to more fully live out your deeply held values and virtues:

HEALTH

HOME

MINISTRY

WORK

RELATIONSHIPS

SPIRITUALITY

PERSONAL GROWTH

What are some hopes and desires you want to bring to God?

Using this diagram, reflect on how fulfilled you feel in each area and put a dot in each section of the diagram to represent the amount of fulfillment you have in that area of your life. The center represents 0 percent fulfillment. The edge represents 100 percent fulfillment.

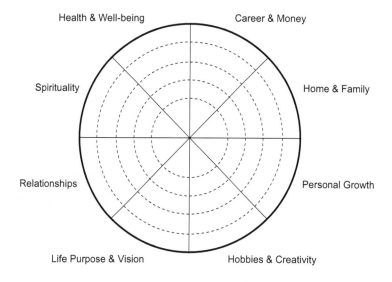

Connect each dot to create a shape on the diagram. As you look at the shape, what are your thoughts or insights?

Write today's date:

Keep your response in this book. You will refer back to this later in your journey.

DAY 3: FIRST THINGS FIRST

But seek first his kingdom and his righteousness, and all these things will be given to you as well.

—MATTHEW 6:33 NIV

Before we proceed further, it is crucial that we clearly understand that the center of our attention should be on things that are dependable, reliable, and trustworthy.

When we put Jesus first and have him at the center of our lives, this is the type of growth we can expect.

Jesus brings us from insecurity to confidently living out who God made us to be. Our trajectory goes from constant fluctuation to plain and straight. Our discernment goes from feeling distorted to clear. Our strength and endurance go from frail and crippled to energized and highly proactive.

But let's say Jesus isn't first. What happens when we start putting things like our romantic relationship, family, money, work, possessions, pleasure, peers, self, and even religion in place of God in our hearts?

PUTTING PEOPLE FIRST

When people are put first, our identity is based on how others treat us, whether they accept us, and what they expect of us. Their opinions of us, whether true or false, heavily influence our image of ourselves.

Our trajectory is limited to what others think is best, and we are molded to their preferences/comfort level. Our progress is based on when they move, where they go, and how far they go.

Discernment is limited by the perspective of the other people and is distorted to meet their wants and desires.

Energy levels are influenced heavily by others. Our strength and endurance are only as strong as our weakest relational link.

Sure, you might be around people who inspire you and encourage you to be better. But they are few and far between.

PUTTING MONEY AND POSSESSIONS FIRST

When money and possessions are put first, our personal self-worth and identity are based on net worth and tangible things.

Our trajectory is based on making profit and protecting what we own. The desire for more wealth and material is never quenched.

Discernment is distorted through the lens of comparative economic standing and making more money.

Strength and endurance rise and fall, depending on how much money we have. Our potential is limited by what we can buy or are payed.

PUTTING PLEASURE FIRST

When pleasure or the self is the center, our identity is constantly shifting due to short-lived moments of feeling good. Our enjoyment is dependent on our environment making us feel good.

Our trajectory is based on "What's in it for me?" and "What will give me the most pleasure?"

Discernment is skewed to benefit the self over others.

Strength and endurance aren't best utilized or even developed when we put pleasure first. Since strength and endurance grow through challenges, the avoidance of situations where we are not in comfort is what prevents us from encountering challenges that grow us.

PUTTING WORK FIRST

When work or religion is the center, our identity is defined by our occupational role. The more we work, the greater the self.

Our trajectory is based on how much work can be accomplished and if our actions will be positively evaluated by peers. Efficiency is made greater than effectiveness.

Discernment is limited and conformed by our role in the workplace.

Strength and endurance are based on position and role, organizational constraints, and the boss's approval.

We can see that allowing any one of these things to influence our heart can lead to a constantly fluctuating life. When God is first, this means that we are trusting our life, ministry, or business to that which is never changing, never biased, and always loving. We are essentially building upon the firmest foundation.

There is that famous quote from Jesus where he talks about building a house on sand versus building a house on the rock (Matthew 7:24–27). The popular lesson people learn is that building a life on what Jesus teaches is like building a house on rock. It's firm, solid, and won't shift or fall apart during the storms in life.

Building on rock is very difficult and extremely time consuming. Rock obviously is very hard and solid, which means digging through it can feel downright impossible. In order to build a house, you need support beams that go several feet underground, and it isn't easy when the ground is literal rock! Plus, constructing a house's foundation takes up 50 percent of the entire time that is spent building a house. Yet the house's foundation determines 100 percent of the longevity of that house.

So if you have a solid foundation set, you have a long-lasting home that seems near impossible to knock down. But many don't want to put the time or energy into digging through that rock. They would rather dig into sand, which is quick and easy! You dig a couple holes, insert a few support beams, and then you are practically halfway done building the house. But you know the story. That house won't last.

In the short term, it might be easier to make decisions in favor of what will make you look good in front of others. Or choose an option that might make you a lot of money. But as we established earlier, these things are constantly fluctuating and won't lead to fulfillment or purpose.

But there is another very valuable lesson that many will not see in the story of building a house on the rock. Many scholars believe that in Jesus's story, He is talking about not building a home in a wadi.

Wadis are deep ravines with high cliff faces that are found in the desert. They are created by water rushing through these ravines, which creates these channels for the water to flow through.

You might think that since it's a desert, there isn't a lot of water in those wadis. And most of the time during the year, you would be correct. But not during a rainy season. When it rains, these wadis are overflowing with rushing floods of water. In fact, the number one cause of death in the desert isn't dehydration or heat exhaustion. Ironically, it's drowning. The reason why is people will be in these wadis when there is rain, and an unexpected flash flood will occur, taking out anything and anyone in them.

Go on YouTube and look up "Flash Floods in Wadi Peres."[3] At around 3:20 in the video, you will see a torrent of rainwater rushing into a wadi. You can even look up "Wadi Flash Flood" and just watch all the videos that come up. These videos make it easy to imagine how devastating it would be to build a house in a wadi while rainwater is crashing through.

(If you would like to hear more about desert imagery in the Bible, I recommend looking up the BEMA Podcast and listening to episode 29 "Images of the Desert — Wadi and En Gedi.")

---

3   Guy Shachar. "Flash Floods in Wadi Peres." YouTube video. May 19, 2014. https://youtu.be/
      yj94OXAg78g?t=138.

You see, Jesus isn't only talking about the structural integrity of rock versus sand. He is also referring to the wise and safe placement of where one's home is built.

If you have a vision and mission that is based on values which are derived from Jesus's teachings, then your actions and impact will endure the test of time. Sure, it might not be easy, just how building a house on rock isn't easy. But it will last, and it will be worth all the time and energy that is invested, unlike the house that is built on sand, which is positioned in dangerous territory.

What you are doing right now is preparing to build on rock. By reading through this book, you are creating a firm foundation which will lead to a fulfilling and impactful life. Even when you do face trials, challenges, and setbacks, God's truth will stand firm and won't change. If anything, the only thing that changes is us and our understanding of God's truth and calling in our life.

The Two Ways

How happy is the man
who does not follow the advice of the wicked
or take the path of sinners
or join a group of mockers!
Instead, his delight is in the LORD's instruction,
and he meditates on it day and night.
He is like a tree planted beside streams of water
that bears its fruit in season,
and whose leaf does not wither.
Whatever he does prospers.
The wicked are not like this;

instead, they are like chaff that the wind blows away.
Therefore the wicked will not survive the judgment,
and sinners will not be in the community of the righteous.
For the LORD watches over the way of the righteous,
but the way of the wicked leads to ruin.

—PSALM 1 HCSB

LET'S FOCUS

If you want to move people, it has to be toward a vision that's positive for them, that taps important values, that gets them something they desire and it has to be presented in a compelling way so that they feel inspired to follow.

—MARTIN LUTHER KING, JR.

Every day, there is a need for us to make the decision to see the world through Christ and to become like Christ in our everyday thoughts and contributions. When we have vision, we can start making progress. It gives us a place to set our sights and helps us know where to be and what direction brings us there.

Unfortunately, every day we are also bombarded with messages and notifications that can distract us from the vision God wants us to see. Just how a magnet can change the direction of where a compass is pointing, outside influences can point our hearts in the wrong direction.

When we lack awareness of what's influencing our deeper motives, it is like building a tower on an unlevel foundation. The higher up the tower goes, the easier it is to see that it's crooked and the more prone it is to collapse. Similarly, the more authority and power we gain, the more apparent any crookedness becomes. If we aren't self-aware, don't see our purpose, and are driven by the wrong values, then we will inevitably collapse.

When the Israelites were in the desert, they reverted to the values of Egypt. They forgot the dissatisfaction that came from being in Egypt and lost sight of the purpose God had given them. When the demands of life exceeded their own willpower, they leaned toward doing what was familiar and easy as opposed to doing what was best. Without vision, they made decisions based on their feelings, moods, and false thoughts.

Although the Israelites were brought out of Egypt... Egypt was not brought out of the Israelites.

Their purpose and identity were lost, and they found themselves wandering for forty years. Wasting not only their own future but also wasting their kid's childhood, they meandered in a desert instead of living in a land flowing with milk and honey.

If we aren't making a conscious effort to refocus on God and don't set our sights on the vision, then we will be swayed to make decisions based on circumstances and feelings instead of Jesus's guidance.

But how does this all fit into the bigger picture of our salvation?

When we start to recognize our thoughts and desires are not always good, we can allow Scripture to determine what we should value most. This method of self-discovery could be used in the process of sanctification as well. By paying attention to where we normally get our values, whether from our family of origin, broader culture, and so on, we might find that these values need to be investigated and often sanctified.

A vision that is built with the values that Jesus taught creates the framework by which we can filter our decisions. This is useful not only on a personal level but on an organizational and even familial level as well. When problems, crises, or even seemingly good opportunities come up, the right values can remind us of the things that matter most. It provides us direction for how to solve problems and discernment for how we should invest our time and energy.

Aligning our values, passions, thoughts, talents, and desires with Jesus will create a more enjoyable and fulfilling life. But the goal isn't merely to have a fun time. The goal is to be more fulfilled, which comes from being more like Christ.

Chapter 2

═══

CULTIVATING

DAY 4: CULTIVATING OUR HEARTS

You are truly amazing if you took the time to go through the first chapter. Even if you didn't fill it out, I want to say you are amazing for simply getting to this point in the book. A lot of people start something without taking the time to follow through on it. For you to be reading this right now means you are the type of person who can follow through to the very end.

But before we continue, I want to encourage those of you who didn't fill out the baseline measurement...

Please go back and fill it out.

By measuring your current state, you are creating a reference point that shows how much you were able to benefit from going on this journey.

When you finish, you can expect to see so much growth that you will look back and say, "Wow! I can't believe I was living my life waaaay back there."

But the only way you can truly recognize and appreciate the amazing transformation that will take place is if you take the time to go through the baseline measurement. So if you didn't already, go back and fill it out.

Now we can continue and talk about what is required in discovering God's calling and having a fruitful life.

Just like a garden, we need fertile ground to work with if we want fruitfulness. To have fertile ground, we need to go through the process of preparing the soil.

Soil, like our heart, can become compact and lose its structure if it is not intentionally maintained. Over time little pockets of air can form and become compressed beneath the surface of the soil. These compressed pockets make it extremely difficult for water and nutrients to move through. As a result, roots can't grow deeper, and the plant is deprived of vital nutrients.

Proper cultivation of soil leads to deeper roots, greater fruit, and long-lasting growth.

In life, we tend to cover up our risky behaviors as though ignoring them, or not acknowledging them, is the means by which to remove them. When we do this, it is like intentionally compressing the dirt in our garden. But the best way to remove these behaviors, and cultivate the dirt, is by addressing and confronting what is beneath the surface.

So let's take our first step in preparing our hearts as we move into cultivating.

BENEFITS OF A CULTIVATED HEART

This is the very perfection of man; to find out his imperfection.
—ST. AUGUSTINE, AD 354 TO AD 430

Hard hearts lead to hard times. Countless times throughout the Bible, we see the troubles that come to those with a hard heart. Inversely, we see the amazing things that God can do with those who have a soft heart.

In the book of Exodus, Pharaoh had a hard heart, and as a result, God sent plagues, destroyed their economy, and allowed Pharaoh and his men to be eaten up by the ocean.

While the Israelites were in the desert, they allowed their hearts to be hardened. On their way to the Promised Land, they broke many agreements with God. This led to the hard-hearted Israelites not making it to the Promised Land.

When our hearts are hardened toward God, we miss out. The condition of our heart influences how deeply God's love grows in us and how fruitful our lives can be. The Pharisees in the New

Testament had hard hearts and squandered the opportunity to personally know God and witness miracles:

In them [the Pharisees] is fulfilled the prophecy of Isaiah:
"'You will be ever hearing but never understanding;
you will be ever seeing but never perceiving.
For this people's heart has become calloused;
they hardly hear with their ears,
and they have closed their eyes.
Otherwise they might see with their eyes,
hear with their ears,
understand with their hearts and turn, and I would heal them."

—MATTHEW 13:14-15 NIV

This quote from Isaiah that Jesus used, was supposed to be a summary of the message he was trying to communicate in his famous story called the "Parable of the Sower," which is found in Matthew 13:1-9, Mark 4:1-9, and Luke 8:4-15.

In this story, there was a man who indiscriminately tossed seed on the ground. Some seeds fell on a path, which was very hard and compact. The seed couldn't take root in the soil, so they were eaten up by birds. Some seeds fell on ground comprised of mostly rocks and little good soil. The seed quickly took root in the areas where there was good soil, but the roots couldn't grow deep, so the plant died. Some seeds fell among thorns that quickly choked out the plants. But the areas where there was good soil produced a crop of thirty, sixty, and one hundred times the amount that was planted.

In this story, the seed represented hearing about God's kingdom, and the soil reflected the state of a person's heart. But it is also a story that shows God's heart too. It reveals how God wants to see growth in everyone, which is why he indiscriminately is throwing seeds. We also see that God wants those seeds to produce not just several more seeds. He says that they will produce a massive amount in return.

God loves to provide abundance and growth. We see it all around us in nature. We can plant one seed and get back hundreds of seeds!

Often, the measure of one's success in ministry is the amount we can grow with the few things we have been given. It isn't about having a lot. It's about doing a lot with what we have. This idea is summarized in this verse:

To those who use well what they are given, even more will be given, and they will have an abundance. But from those who do nothing, even what little they have will be taken away.

—MATTHEW 25:29 NLT

If God's word can't take root in our lives, then we will miss out on experiencing the abundance that can come from planting what few things God has given us.

Proper cultivation of our heart is the first step to allowing God to produce in us a purposeful and fruitful life that is well defined by vision and mission! Cultivation of the heart brings more productivity and effectiveness with what few things we have.

Thoroughly cultivating our heart requires time, patience, and getting our hands dirty. It involves identifying and removing the things that will prevent or hinder God's word from growing in us.

Although most would like to get straight to planting, have a beautiful garden, a thriving career, an impactful ministry, or a meaningful life, rushing through the cultivation process can lead to a lot of hard work, time, and resources that produce little and possibly nothing in return.

That is why I want to challenge you to complete it thoroughly, but don't worry about doing it perfectly. Simply trust the process, and you will complete this section in no time.

DAY 5: GETTING OUR HANDS DIRTY

No discipline is enjoyable while it is happening—it's painful! But afterward there will be a peaceful harvest of right living for those who are trained in this way.

—HEBREWS 12:11 NLT

How often do you make the time to step back and ask, "Is the life that I am living worth the things that I'm sacrificing?"

Imagine working your whole life to try and achieve the thing you desired most only to get there and find that no purpose, joy, peace, fulfillment, or fruitfulness was there? It would be like spending an entire summer starting a vegetable garden only to find out none of the seeds you planted could produce vegetables.

As a kid, I used to believe that every tree had the potential to be an apple tree. I remember looking at the trees in our backyard and thinking, "If apples come from trees, and these are trees, then apples must be able to grow from them."

This of course was a logical fallacy, which is a flaw in reasoning. You and I both know that apples don't grow from every kind of tree.

But imagine if I had depended on apples growing from those trees. Imagine if I had devoted my whole life to the eventual production of apples from a tree that could produce no fruit? It would be a tragedy.

Since I am older and wiser than I was as a child, I have more information and understanding of how the real world works. I can see why my sincere effort to get apples from my backyard was fruitless.

Fortunately, the things that God plants in our lives always have the potential to be fruitful. But before we can receive anything from God, we first need to be sure we are able to receive the seeds He wants to plant in our hearts.

As we learned earlier, a hard heart can prevent seeds from growing deep roots. Even if we have the right seeds, we might not have the right environment to grow them.

Just as I had a logical fallacy in my beliefs for how apples are produced, we can very easily have logical fallacies in our beliefs for how to produce fruit in our own life.

When it comes to having purpose, we should be aware of the condition of our heart. We should know if we are in a state that can lead us to fruitfulness or desolation.

The best way to avoid spending our life sitting under a fruitless tree expecting food, or planting a garden and having nothing to harvest, is to start by cultivating. This means we are to turn through the dirt and remove the things that can harden our hearts and lead us, our ministry, or our business in the wrong direction.

Examples of things that can lead us in the wrong direction include seeking wealth, pleasure, and status. Although God may provide us wealth, allow us to enjoy good things, and elevate us socially, we are not to place these things above God. Having these things as the source from which we try to find our purpose or meaning will only lead to an unfulfilled life.

To begin the cultivating process, we are going to read through and study the wisdom found in the book of Ecclesiastes. It was written by King Solomon, who is said to have been fabulously wealthy, wise, and influential. The perspective the author takes is of someone who has it all. But as they sit back and examine all they have done and own, they find that many of the things such as wealth, health, materialism, and power ultimately lead to unfulfillment.

So what is it that brings about fulfillment? How should we use our time? Where should our focus be?

This book will shed some light to answer those questions.

Some find the book of Ecclesiastes to be depressing due to its nihilistic nature. But when reading Ecclesiastes, try to view it as though you're receiving advice from:

- A mentor who's further in the journey than you are

- A firm teacher who guides you through what you got wrong on a test

- A strong athletic coach giving you challenging training because they see the hidden talent within you

- A wise parent who enjoys seeing what you accomplished but then asks, "What's next?"

You may have encountered one or all of these types of people. They are often older, wiser, speak very bluntly, have a powerful voice, tolerate zero BS, and are intimidating or borderline frightening.

But deep down, they are not trying to hurt us; they are trying to help mature us by doing four things:

1. Strengthen the areas where we are weak rather than ignoring our weaknesses

2. Challenge us based on the potential *they* see in us, not the way *we* see ourselves

3. Encourage gradual growth while discouraging stagnation

4. Lead us toward what is right rather than what is comfortable

The book of Ecclesiastes is these four people and does those four things. Its wisdom cuts right to the heart of the false paradigms and broken foundations we may be building our lives, our careers, or our relationships on. But I can assure you that by the time you get done reading it, the wisdom from Ecclesiastes will help to:

- Properly orient our hearts *away* from things that don't last (Ecclesiastes 2:9–11)

- Get us out of the rat race (Ecclesiastes 1:3, 8)

- Give us a grander perspective of our life beyond just the here and now (Ecclesiastes 5:18–20)

Like a rotary tiller, Ecclesiastes will cut through the surface, exposing and digging out any hardened paradigms or life goals that are in our hearts.

If you do seek things like wealth, pleasures, status, and a stable career, it's best to recognize it. To ignore does not mean to eliminate. But don't be ashamed; we all experience some form of attachment to one, if not all, of these things. But this section will work to expose and remove those attachments.

CULTIVATING THE HEART (EXERCISE)

This will be a crucial first step on the journey to discovering God's calling. Don't overthink your responses, but do take your time.

I recommend you watch the YouTube video "The Book of Ecclesiastes" by the Bible Project. You can watch the video by scanning the QR code here. (To scan the QR code, open the camera on your smartphone. Then view the code through your camera, and a link should appear)

This video makes for great supplementary material that will add to your depth and understanding of Ecclesiastes, which will allow you to get more out of this section as well.

Here is a general overview of what you will be doing as you go through the text. Each day will feature different themes found in the book of Ecclesiastes. After you read through the verses, you will follow the order of these steps:

1. Write down two to four verses that stand out to you while you read: be aware of any verses that inspire you, or create a sense of disruption inside you.

2. Describe, in your own words, the wisdom the verse communicates to you.

3. Tag each description based on the theme or message it conveys to you.

    A. For example, if you find that one of your descriptions talks about leadership, you could tag that as "Leadership."

    B. If a description touches upon several messages or themes, write down the two or three tags that best illustrate the message.

Disclaimer: Not every verse or theme found in Ecclesiastes could be included in this book. If you would like to get the most out of this section, then you should read through the entire book of Ecclesiastes!

ECCLESIASTES 1

3 What do people get for all their hard work under the sun?... 8 No matter how much we see, we are never satisfied. No matter how much we hear, we are not content.

ECCLESIASTES 2

8 I had everything a man could desire! ...

9 I became greater than all who had lived in Jerusalem before me, and my wisdom never failed me. 10 Anything I wanted, I would take. I denied myself no pleasure. I even found great pleasure in hard work, a reward for all my labors. 11 But as I looked at everything I had worked so hard to accomplish, it was all so meaningless—like chasing the wind. There was nothing really worthwhile anywhere. ...

21 Some people work wisely with knowledge and skill, then must leave the fruit of their efforts to someone who hasn't worked for it.

ECCLESIASTES 4

8 This is the case of a man who is all alone, without a child or a brother, yet who works hard to gain as much wealth as he can. But then he asks himself, "Who am I working for? Why am I giving up so much pleasure now?" It is all so meaningless and depressing.

9 Two people are better off than one, for they can help each other succeed. 10 If one person falls, the other can reach out and help. But someone who falls alone is in real trouble.

1. Verse _:_

   Description:

   Tag:

2. Verse _:_

   Description:

   Tag:

3. Verse _:_

   Description:

   Tag:

4. Verse _:_

Description:

Tag:

DAY 6
ECCLESIASTES 4

4 Then I observed that most people are motivated to success because they envy their neighbors. But this, too, is meaningless—like chasing the wind.

5 "Fools fold their idle hands, leading them to ruin."

6 And yet, "Better to have one handful with quietness than two handfuls with hard work and chasing the wind."

ECCLESIASTES 5

10 Those who love money will never have enough. How meaningless to think that wealth brings true happiness!

11 The more you have, the more people come to help you spend it. So what good is wealth—except perhaps to watch it slip through your fingers!

12 People who work hard sleep well, whether they eat little or much. But the rich seldom get a good night's sleep.

13 There is another serious problem I have seen under the sun. Hoarding riches harms the saver... 15 We all come to the end of our lives as naked and empty-handed as on the day we were born. We can't take our riches with us.

18 Even so, I have noticed one thing, at least, that is good. It is good for people to eat, drink, and enjoy their work under the sun during the short life God has given them, and to accept their lot in life. 19 And it is a good thing to receive wealth from God and the good health to enjoy it. To enjoy your work and accept your lot in life—this is indeed a gift from God. 20 God keeps such people so busy enjoying life that they take no time to brood over the past.

ECCLESIASTES 6

3 A man might have a hundred children and live to be very old. But if he finds no satisfaction in life and doesn't even get a decent burial, it would have been better for him to be born dead... 6 He might live a thousand years twice over but still not find contentment. And since he must die like everyone else—well, what's the use?

9 Enjoy what you have rather than desiring what you don't have. Just dreaming about nice things is meaningless—like chasing the wind.

ECCLESIASTES 9

10 Whatever you do, do well. For when you go to the grave, there will be no work or planning or knowledge or wisdom.

1. Verse _:_

    Description:

    Tag:

2. Verse _:_

    Description:

    Tag:

3. Verse _:_

    Description:

Tag:

4. Verse _:_

   Description:

   Tag:

DAY 7
ECCLESIASTES 3

1 For everything there is a season, a time for every activity under heaven...

11 God has made everything beautiful for its own time. He has planted eternity in the human heart, but even so, people cannot see the whole scope of God's work from beginning to end.

ECCLESIASTES 5

2 Don't make rash promises, and don't be hasty in bringing matters before God. After all, God is in heaven, and you are here on earth. So let your words be few...

4 When you make a promise to God, don't delay in following through, for God takes no pleasure in fools. Keep all the prom-

ises you make to him. 5 It is better to say nothing than to make a promise and not keep it.

ECCLESIASTES 9

11 I have observed something else under the sun. The fastest runner doesn't always win the race, and the strongest warrior doesn't always win the battle. The wise sometimes go hungry, and the skillful are not necessarily wealthy. And those who are educated don't always lead successful lives. It is all decided by chance, by being in the right place at the right time.

ECCLESIASTES 10

17 Happy is the land whose king is a noble leader and whose leaders feast at the proper time to gain strength for their work, not to get drunk.

ECCLESIASTES 11

4 Farmers who wait for perfect weather never plant. If they watch every cloud, they never harvest.

6 Plant your seed in the morning and keep busy all afternoon, for you don't know if profit will come from one activity or another—or maybe both.

9 Young people, it's wonderful to be young! Enjoy every minute of it. Do everything you want to do; take it all in. But remember that you must give an account to God for everything you do. 10

So refuse to worry, and keep your body healthy. But remember that youth, with a whole life before you, is meaningless.

ECCLESIASTES 12

1 Don't let the excitement of youth cause you to forget your Creator. Honor him in your youth before you grow old and say, "Life is not pleasant anymore."

1. Verse _:_

    Description:

    Tag:

2. Verse _:_

    Description:

    Tag:

3. Verse _:_

   Description:

   Tag:

4. Verse _:_

   Description:

   Tag:

DAY 8
ECCLESIASTES 1

17 I set out to learn everything from wisdom to madness and folly. But I learned firsthand that pursuing all this is like chasing the wind.

ECCLESIASTES 4

13 It is better to be a poor but wise youth than an old and foolish king who refuses all advice.

5 Better to be criticized by a wise person than to be praised by a fool...

7 Extortion turns wise people into fools, and bribes corrupt the heart.

8 Finishing is better than starting. Patience is better than pride. 9 Control your temper, for anger labels you a fool. 10 Don't long for "the good old days." This is not wise...

12 Wisdom and money can get you almost anything, but only wisdom can save your life.

13 Accept the way God does things, for who can straighten what he has made crooked? 14 Enjoy prosperity while you can, but when hard times strike, realize that both come from God. Remember that nothing is certain in this life...

16 Don't be too good or too wise! Why destroy yourself? 17 On the other hand, don't be too wicked either. Don't be a fool! Why die before your time? 18 Pay attention to these instructions, for anyone who fears God will avoid both extremes...

20 Not a single person on earth is always good and never sins...

29 But I did find this: God created people to be virtuous, but they have each turned to follow their own downward path.

ECCLESIASTES 10

10 Using a dull ax requires great strength, so sharpen the blade. That's the value of wisdom; it helps you succeed. 11 If a snake bites before you charm it, what's the use of being a snake charmer?

ECCLESIASTES 12

13 Here now is my final conclusion: Fear God and obey his commands, for this is everyone's duty. 14 God will judge us for everything we do, including every secret thing, whether good or bad.

1. Verse _:_

   Description:

   Tag:

2. Verse _:_

   Description:

   Tag:

3. Verse _:_

   Description:

   Tag:

4. Verse _:_

   Description:

   Tag:

Bonus: Once you have tagged your notes, get a separate piece of paper and compile all the descriptions with the same tag to form a short paragraph. For example, all the descriptions that may have been tagged as "Leadership" will be put together to form a short paragraph about leadership. All the notes tagged "Giving" will be put together to create a paragraph on giving.

If a description has more than one tag, it can be used again in multiple paragraphs. For example, a note that is tagged as "Leadership" and "Giving" can be included in both the leadership and giving paragraph.

These paragraphs will be vital down the road. We will be referring to these notes later in this book. So having these paragraphs will serve as a quick refresher of what you learned in Ecclesiastes.

When you have the paragraphs written out, you can fold the piece of paper and insert it right here in the book for later.

CULTIVATING WRAP-UP

Experience is not what happens to you. It is what you do with what happens to you. Don't waste your pain; use it to help others.

—RICK WARREN, *THE PURPOSE DRIVEN LIFE: WHAT ON EARTH AM I HERE FOR?*

Many find the book of Ecclesiastes difficult to internalize due to its nihilistic style of writing and how it says things like, *"For death is the destiny of every person, and the living should take this to heart."* (Ecclesiastes 7:2)

Although this may seem bleak, God has used death to bring freedom and new life for all of us through Jesus's death and resurrection. Death is no longer the end. God has turned it into a tool that can bring us liberation and renewal.

Remember, Jesus offers us new life when we let go of the life we may be desperately holding on to. Therefore, trust Jesus. Go in the direction he is leading you and take to heart the values, lessons, and wisdom he taught.

Here are some verses on the subject that you can meditate on.

If you try to hang on to your life, you will lose it. But if you give up your life for my sake, you will save it.

—MATTHEW 16:25 NLT

I tell you the truth, unless a kernel of wheat is planted in the soil and dies, it remains alone. But its death will produce many new kernels—a plentiful harvest of new lives.

—JOHN 12:24 NLT

Therefore, if anyone is in Christ, the new creation has come: The old has gone, the new is here!

—2 CORINTHIANS 5:17 NIV

I will give them an undivided heart and put a new spirit in them; I will remove from them their heart of stone and give them a heart of flesh.

—EZEKIEL 11:19 NIV

You were taught, with regard to your former way of life, to put off your old self, which is being corrupted by its deceitful desires; to be made new in the attitude of your minds; and to put on the new self, created to be like God in true righteousness and holiness.

—EPHESIANS 4:22-24 NIV

Chapter 3

DIGGING

DAY 9: GETTING DEEP

Let me say, Congratulations for making it to this point in the book. By going through the cultivation section and filling out the exercise section completely, you are showing just how truly serious you are about discerning the vision and mission that God wants you to see. To be at this point means you are someone who puts in the hard work because you want great results in your life. I'm truly pleased with you for what progress you have made.

The process you went through in the previous section has begun to establish the foundation for creating a fertile heart that can produce purpose. We have started to overturn the top of the soil, which will allow for the seeds that are planted later to take root and produce a good fruit!

Cultivating our heart aided in identifying and removing the surface-level desires that don't allow for true fruitfulness and fulfillment. During this process, you may have found that the wisdom from Ecclesiastes dug deep and hit some hard spots in your heart.

For some, these hard spots were resolved through cultivating. But for many, the cultivation process may have just scratched the surface of something that's more problematic than just "compact dirt." This section will be devoted to digging up those hard spots.

As you continue, I would like to challenge you to stay consistent with how much you have been reading. This next section will stir up emotions that might try to distract you from completing the chapter. But remember, preparing the soil in a garden takes time, and it involves getting some dirt under your nails. So embrace it. Soon enough, you will be feeling as though you are growing by leaps and bounds!

DIGGING OUT THE HARD STUFF

[Jesus] replied, "Every plant that my heavenly Father has not planted will be pulled up by the roots."

—MATTHEW 15:13 NIV

Every year, about 73,000 amputations are performed on the lower limbs of those with diabetes.[4]

What's interesting is that none of these amputations were the result of a traumatic injury or a major accident. They were caused by a ravenous, yet simple to cure, infection that went untreated. Although it is possible to have cured the infection with antibiotics and eliminate the need for amputation, these men and women didn't seek out treatment. But why would someone with diabetes not get treatment if their body is being eaten away by an infection?

Dr. Lawrence Kassan DPM, Syracuse University graduate and board-certified surgical care specialist of the foot and ankle, says that he encounters this a lot with diabetic patients. The reason why patients with diabetes don't seek treatment for infections in limbs, such as their feet, is because they don't realize that their feet are infected. This is due to something called "diabetic neuropathy," which is nerve damage that can cause numbness and loss of sensation in the feet, legs, and hands. This nerve damage occurs when blood sugar levels are too high, which is more likely to happen to those with diabetes. Since the nerve damage prevents people with diabetes from feeling anything in their limbs, they may get a cut on an area, such as the foot, and not realize it even happened.

When a cut is not acknowledged and not properly cleaned, the cut is susceptible to getting infected. Over time, the infection

---

4   Centers for Disease Control and Prevention, "National Diabetes Statistics Report," Centers for Disease Control and Prevention, February 24, 2018. http://www.cdc.gov/diabetes/data/statistics/2014statisticsreport.html.

slowly eats away at the flesh without the person even noticing anything is wrong. By the time the individual does notice the infection, the only thing doctors can do is remove the infected area. This sometimes means the amputation of a toe, a foot, or even a whole leg!

It's important to note that it's not the diabetes or the diabetic neuropathy that causes lower-limb amputations. Rather, it's the inability to recognize that there is an infection.

If we neglect to notice what is buried in us, it is like neglecting to notice an infection on our feet. Therefore, we need to dig deep and address what may be hindering us from further growth in our life and ministry.

Most often, the things that prevent us from growing are our own self-defeating or self-sabotaging behaviors and beliefs. They are like large dense rocks buried deep in our hearts. When you encounter this rock, self-sabotage begins to ensue.

Dr. Gay Hendricks, writer and teacher with a PhD in psychology from Stanford University, talks about these "rocks" as being upper-limit problems in his book *The Big Leap*. From Hendricks's experience working with patients, he found that people have within them an "inner thermostat" that determines how much love, success, and creativity an individual will allow for themselves. When that "thermostat setting" is exceeded, the individual may subconsciously act out in a way that will cause them to drop them back into the old setting that they're familiar with. Most often, these behaviors are self-sabotaging in nature.

Most, if not all of us, have some deeply buried values and beliefs that are obstructing our development. These deeply buried values or beliefs are barriers that, if not addressed, will further hinder how much we'll allow God to grow and give us.

In the "Parable of the Sower," Jesus talks about the seed that grows quickly but has shallow roots. Those roots couldn't grow any deeper because there was rock under the surface of the dirt that prevented greater growth. Since the roots are shallow, the plant won't last long. As soon as any problems arise, the plant withers and dies.

You might have large rocks, nonbiodegradable waste, or even ravenous weeds buried under the surface, and you may not even notice they're there. These things may not cause any immediate negative influences on your garden's growth. You'll see progress and plants will take root. But down the road, these things that are beneath the surface will be a barrier that is going to always hinder the depth and longevity of your development.

Sure, I want your ministry to grow. Sure, I want you to see growth in your life. But what we really should want is to have those things grow *and* last.

These rocks weren't recently buried in your life. They were put there a long time ago and got further and further buried as time went on. You may only have one or two of the false rocks that we'll talk about later in this section. But all these buried barriers have something in common: they appear foundational to the integrity of your garden, but in reality, they are not.

When you remove these false beliefs, you'll feel a new sense of freedom because it, quite literally, frees up space for God to work in you. The whole process starts by simply considering the possibility that you have at least one of these barriers buried in you.

If we want to provide the best environment for the seeds that God plants, then now is the time to dig deeper beneath the surface. This section will help to identify and dig up the rocks, the hard spots, in our heart.

DANGERS OF A ROCKY FOUNDATION

It may sound odd, but there are many who don't want to be more successful or more responsible.

This avoidance of success or accomplishment can be rooted in a variety of false ideas or anxieties. One of which can be due to a fear of inevitably failing. Subconsciously, some will hold themselves back from reaching that next level just so they can avoid the possibility of being knocked down.

What happens is we grow up seeing people get more and more successful, going higher and higher in life, just to fall the hardest. We become accustomed to the amount of success we've already had and come to be uncomfortable, or feel ill-equipped, to handle more. It is seen time and time again in the Bible where characters gain a lot of responsibility or overcome a challenge just to fall when they are at their highest point.

- Noah got drunk right off the boat (Genesis 9:21)

- Moses hits the rock before going into the Promised Land (Numbers 20:21)

- Gideon creates an idol from the gold won in battles (Judges 8:27)

- Sampson becomes more promiscuous, violent, and arrogant (Judges 13–16)

- The Israelites languish in the desert for forty years (Numbers 32:13)

- King Saul takes it upon himself to do the sacrifice (1 Samuel 13)

- David sleeps with a married woman (2 Samuel 11)

- Solomon marries outside of the nation (1 Kings 11:1–11)

But what we fail to recognize is that the downward spirals of these successful figures were caused by internal self-sabotaging behaviors. None of them were external, meaning these individuals were the ones that caused their own downfall.

These people experienced an elevation in their social status, financial security, influence, and wisdom, which was apparently too much for them to manage.

Before these biblical figures could reach their fullest potential and calling in life, they knocked themselves down. As they reached new heights, the faults in their foundational beliefs became more prominent.

Like a foundation that is slightly uneven, the higher up a structure is built, the more drastic the acute angles become. Only as the building gets higher does the unleveled foundation become more problematic to the structural integrity of the building.

But this doesn't mean it is impossible to experience an abundance of joy, peace, and growth. These are things that Jesus offers for us to have even when we are facing challenges in life.

So if we can experience a fruitful life of peace, joy, and growth, then what can we do to remove these deeply buried beliefs that lead to self-sabotaging behaviors?

First, you need to know that these deeply buried beliefs do not belong in you or your garden. Although some of these beliefs may have been there since childhood, you need to understand that they were not always in you. They were placed there early on and got buried deeper and deeper as time passed.

It is like that famous saying about how God bringing the Israelites out of Egypt was the easy part. The hard part would be to bring Egypt out of the Israelites.

What this means is that over the hundreds of years that the Israelites spent in Egypt, over time, the Egyptian culture began to influence the hearts of the Israelites. Although God managed to remove His people from Egypt, He now needed to remove the Egyptian influence from His people.

Once you realize that these buried beliefs are false, then you need to consciously focus on them in order to break them apart. All it takes is having a conscious awareness of which beliefs you have in you, then give them to God. You may need to spend a lot of time prayerfully examining the rocks that are buried. But soon you'll begin to realize how they were simply barriers preventing you from having greater growth and more fruitfulness in your life, ministry, or relationships.

DAY 10: REMOVING THE ROCKS

When it comes to pursuing one's calling, there are three common rocks that will hinder you. These rocks can prevent your life and ministry from flourishing and will lead to self-sabotaging the good things that are growing.

As you are reading, remain aware of which ones may resonate with your life.

BIG ROCK #1: ONLY THOSE WHO ARE PERFECT CAN DO OR BE USED FOR GREAT THINGS.

Before explaining this belief, it's important to note that there is one of two polar extremes that accompany this perspective.

The first extreme is that we think so little of ourselves that we avoid stepping into our calling. Basically, we believe that God can't use us because we are too fundamentally flawed.

When we view our life through this extreme, we make excuses for why we should avoid big opportunities to grow relationally, vocationally, and spiritually. We don't think we deserve more and/or don't think we are capable of handling greater responsibility. When we are praised for a job well done, we are either quick to point out our flaws or are unable to accept the compliment internally. When we are elevated to a greater role, we feel like an imposter because our flaws influence our perception of ourselves more than our accomplishments do. Our eyes are fixed on our past mistakes instead of God or the talents God has given us. Therefore, we only accept opportunities where we can get average results, and we rarely leverage our talents during occasions where we may perform exceptionally well.

The person who believes they need to be perfect is essentially driving through life with their foot on the gas and the brake at the same time. They can go faster but never do. Their foot on the brake becomes a self-imposed limit on how far and how fast they will go. When they do try to go faster, the hindering effects of the brake are felt, but the individual fails to recognize that the brake is being pressed. Even if the foot is lifted off the brake, they'd be too afraid to speed up and not confident enough to drive at faster speeds. Ultimately, this person doesn't get to the destination because their lack of belief in themselves and in God causes them to slow down far too frequently.

On the other end of the spectrum, we can have the opposite occur. The second extreme is that we think so highly of ourselves that we develop an overinflated ego. Instead of thinking we can't do great things because we aren't perfect, we think that we are perfect or superior to others because we *have* done great things. This person is so focused on going further that they miss the greater calling God has for them.

Viewing oneself as perfect/superior means that accomplishments and social status, whether earned or given, are perceived to be direct measures of our being better than others. Good behavior and kind acts are done for superficial needs or social leveraging. Our lives are drawn toward making decisions that can feed our ego and improve our social status. We become less reliant on God, believing that we can handle everything on our own. We even ignore God's calling because we believe our vision for our life is better than God's infinitely greater purpose. We see ourselves as better than others and grow less aware of our natural limitations.

The person who believes they are perfect/superior is like a person who is speeding on the highway. They assume their destination is greater than others', so they drive over the speed limit to get to their destination. They acknowledge that it's important to follow the law, but they only abide by it when convenient. This person is quick to condemn those who don't follow the rules and is easily agitated by any small inconvenience caused by others. This person is so focused on getting ahead that they are at greater risk of burning out, getting in an accident, hurting others, and ultimately missing their destination.

Biblical Examples of Big Rock #1

Both extremes of the perfection belief are very damaging relationally. When we think little of ourselves, we are hurting our relationship with our inner selves. When we think greater of ourselves, then we are hurting our relationship with others. But the one relationship we damage most is our relationship with God.

Both extremes view God as being too weak.

The first extreme of thinking little of our self is essentially making the claim, "I am too flawed to be used by God. Therefore, God is too weak to use someone like me."

The second extreme of thinking too highly of our self is making the claim, "I know more of what's best for me than God does.

Therefore, God is too limited to understand what can bring me fulfillment and meet my needs."

Whether we think we are weak or strong, we aren't meant to live life based on our own ways. Rather, we are to simply follow Jesus's way, which isn't easy or simple, but it is a straightforward decision that involves following and trusting him.

Then Jesus said to his disciples, "If any of you wants to be my follower, you must give up your own way, take up your cross, and follow me. If you try to hang on to your life, you will lose it. But if you give up your life for my sake, you will save it. And what do you benefit if you gain the whole world but lose your own soul? Is anything worth more than your soul?"

—MATTHEW 16:24-26 NLT

To break apart the rock of perfectionism, you should remember this saying: God doesn't call the qualified; He qualifies those whom He calls.

Peter thought of himself as not being worthy enough to follow Jesus. Early on in his interactions with Jesus, Peter tells Jesus to leave him because he is "a sinful man." But Jesus had bigger plans and knew he could make Peter into one of the pillars of God's church (Luke 5:8-11).

Jeremiah was afraid to follow God's calling. He was scared, doubted his ability to speak, and felt inept because of his young age (Jeremiah 1:4-9).

Gideon, despite being afraid, needing multiple signs from God, and believing he was "the least in [his] family," he trusted God and did his best to follow God's calling on his life (Judges 7:11–16).

Abraham and Sarah could have put the brakes on where God was leading them. They had the excuses of being too old and not knowing the land where God was calling them to, but they still had faith in God (Hebrews 11:8–12).

Moses doubted his own ability to be used by God. At that point in his life, Moses felt like an outsider to both the Egyptians and the Hebrews. After news had spread that he had killed an Egyptian, Moses ran and hid in the desert, taking on a new life. He was mocked by Hebrew people and was probably seen as a fugitive in the eyes of the Egyptians. Although Moses wasn't born Egyptian and didn't grow up in the Hebrew culture, he used to be able to appeal to both Hebrews and Egyptians. But now his reputation was tainted on both sides. Moses understood the magnitude and necessity to face Pharaoh and free the Hebrews, but he didn't feel qualified or confident in his speaking capabilities. Moses felt there was no reason why either group should even listen to him, so he insisted that someone else take his place (Exodus 3:11–14; 4:1, 10–15).

Despite all the excuses Moses made, God still wanted to use Moses and was able to. God met Moses's concerns, and it was up to Moses to step into his calling and trust God (Hebrews 11:24–28).

There's nothing wrong with not feeling adequate or having 100 percent confidence in one's self. What we see from these stories is that God doesn't come expecting us to be the best. He comes expecting us to be faithful.

But what if we trust so much in our own abilities that we can't see the point of relying on God?

Well, we read about a man in the New Testament who had more confidence in who he was than in who God is. This man was named Saul, who later changed his name to Paul. Despite having all the credentials and accomplishments to view himself as being above others, Paul chose to put it all behind him in order to follow Jesus's way and not his own way. He could see the infinitely greater call and purpose that comes from following Jesus. Paul said it like this:

We rely on what Christ Jesus has done for us. We put no confidence in human effort, though I could have confidence in my own effort if anyone could. Indeed, if others have reason for confidence in their own efforts, I have even more!

I was circumcised when I was eight days old. I am a pure-blooded citizen of Israel and a member of the tribe of Benjamin—a real Hebrew if there ever was one! I was a member of the Pharisees, who demand the strictest obedience to the Jewish law. I was so zealous that I harshly persecuted the church. And as for righteousness, I obeyed the law without fault.

I once thought these things were valuable, but now I consider them worthless because of what Christ has done. Yes, everything else is worthless when compared with the infinite value of knowing Christ Jesus my Lord. For his sake I have discarded everything else, counting it all as garbage, so that I could gain Christ and become one with him. I no longer count on my own righteousness through obeying the law; rather, I become righteous through faith in Christ. For God's way of making us right with himself depends on faith.

—PHILIPPIANS 3:3–9 NLT

If we pursue a vision that we feel we can do without God, then it means the vision we are chasing is too small. If we are pursuing a vision that is too big for us, we may feel afraid to even step into it.

However, when God places in our hearts a dream and vision that is so big, so impossibly positive, and so impactful that it would be impossible for us to do it on our own, then it means it is a vision from God. It means we will need to be close to God, but it also means God wants us to be close to Him. Because if we are to get to the end, being close to God is the only way to make it.

You did not choose me, but I chose you and appointed you so that you might go and bear fruit—fruit that will last—and so that whatever you ask in my name the Father will give you.

—JOHN 15:16 NIV

REFLECTION QUESTIONS

Answer these questions below about how your buried barriers might be creating hesitation to step into your calling:

- How might my view of perfection be preventing me from receiving God's vision for my life?

- How might this view of perfection lead to behaviors that sabotage future growth in my life?

- Which Biblical example stood out to you the most? What about this example caused it to stand out?

DAY 11

BIG ROCK #2: FOLLOWING GOD'S CALLING WILL LEAD TO DETACHMENT FROM SOCIETY AND LOSS OF ALL POSSESSIONS.

Basically, this is the lone monk mentality. Thinking that following God's calling for your life means you will be living up in the mountains or out in the woods all alone with no belongings. This is a tough false belief to dig out for a few reasons.

The first reason why this belief is difficult to remove is because there are various accounts in Scripture where people who follow God's calling end up in a desert or lose all their possessions. This has led to many Christians believing that God is always going to strip us of our relationships and possessions (which is not true, and I'll explain why later).

The second is that when we think we'll lose everything and gain nothing by following Jesus, it makes sense that some may turn away from that option.

If we believe that it is fundamentally bad to own anything or to have relationships, then the accumulation of wealth, responsibility, and any form of possessions will lead to feelings of guilt, shame, and self-sabotage.

I'm not pushing the prosperity gospel. The Bible does say that we shouldn't treasure material wealth (Matthew 6:19–21 and 1 Timothy 6:17).

But when it comes to being in a position of having great influence or income, the problem doesn't stem from merely having power or wealth. The problems come from not properly managing the things we were given.

Neither extreme is correct. Having no relationships or possession isn't God's way. But seeking to only amass possessions or strive to please others isn't God's way either.

We need to remember that God wants us to enjoy the things he blesses us with. Also, our intrinsic worth isn't in the possessions we own or the social status we have among the people around us. Our worth is based on who God is, and who we are: God's children.

Biblical Examples of Big Rock #2

If you are worried to follow God's call because you are afraid you will lose what you currently are clinging onto. Just know that there is much more God wants to give you, which might require you to let go of the things you are grasping so tightly.

There are moments in the Bible when God's people went, or were sent, into the wilderness. There are also moments in the Bible when God's people gave up, or lost, everything they once valued.

But these were merely necessary steps in the process of becoming the people God was calling them to be.

When someone went through the desert, God transformed them into a person who could truly step into their calling. The early Israelites who left Egypt and went into the desert weren't allowing themselves to be transformed by God. Since they lost faith in God and held onto their old values, they couldn't step into the Promised Land and ended up dying in the wilderness.

In contrast, the Godly people who did give up what they once thought was valuable *so that* they could receive a truly fruitful life were able to step into the Promised Land. They ended up having greater riches and purpose than they could have ever achieved prior. We read about this pattern happening time and time again.

Abraham moved to a place he had never been, and left everything behind, so that he would receive the promise God gave him. His result? The nation of Israel and, eventually, the birth of Jesus.

Joseph telling everyone about the vision God gave him led to him losing everything, becoming a literal slave, being falsely convicted as a rapist, and being thrown in jail. His result? Joseph grew into the man who was able to handle the power and influence that came from being put in charge of all of Egypt.

Moses left all his influence, inherited wealth, and the comforts of living with Pharaoh's family behind. He became nothing and lived in the desert, caring for sheep. His result? Moses got to experience being in God's presence and was transformed into a courageous man. He soon was able to confidently confront the most powerful person in the world, Pharaoh. Moses was able to bring the Israelites out of Egypt and laid the foundation that Joshua would build off of when bringing the Israelites into the Promised Land.

Israel as a nation was in the desert for forty years before they could even enter the Promised Land. They lived in tents, were constantly moving, and owned no land. Their result? They were able to fully trust God once again. Those who were negatively influencing the nation had died off. They won the Promised Land from literal giants, and they got to enjoy a life with God as their king in a land that was flowing with milk and honey.

After Elijah listened to God and confronted Ahab, Elijah's life was threatened. So he went into the desert, fearing he would be murdered otherwise. His result? He was able to witness three amazing miracles. The first was that God provided Elijah with food that was brought to him by birds. The second was witnessing the miracle of the flour and olive oil that wouldn't run out for the woman and her son. The third was bringing a woman's son back to life.

After God told Samuel to anoint David to be the future king of Israel, David eventually found himself in the desert in order to avoid being killed by King Saul. His result? David's true heart and character were revealed, thus proving his worthiness of being the next king.

Daniel faced adversity after adversity for keeping God's commandments. By obeying God, he was thrown into a den of hungry lions and tossed into a furnace with his closest friends. His result? The lions did not eat him, and his friends did not burn, and they were able to inspire the exiled Israelite nation and write out prophecies that would keep the people inspired for generations to come.

Jesus was in the desert for forty days without food or water and had a literal encounter with the devil. During his persecution, he was abandoned and sentenced to death. His result? Jesus showed us the power that comes from knowledge of Scripture, trust in God, and having our identity found in God. Jesus left the desert, led the most impactful ministry in history, and freed us from the grip of death itself!

Don't confuse what's happening here. Following God didn't bring these people into suffering. Following God allowed them to get through the suffering, thus making them into Godly people. They followed God's call on their life, showing they were responsible enough to be blessed with more.

But then again, this idea of going through suffering has led to a lot of misunderstanding about what it means to follow God's calling in our life, which leads us to our next rock.

REFLECTION QUESTIONS

Answer these questions about how your buried barriers might be creating hesitation to step into your calling:

- Where might my attachment to society and possessions be taking up space in my heart to value what God values?

- How might this view of being void of relationships or possessions lead to behaviors that sabotage future growth in my life?

- Which biblical example stood out to you the most? What about this example caused it to stand out?

DAY 12

BIG ROCK #3: YOU NEED TO SUFFER IN YOUR WORK IN ORDER TO PLEASE GOD.

This is another rock that is hard to break for similar reasons found in the previous false belief.

Although we read in the Bible that people go through struggles and suffer while pursuing God's calling, God's plan, and our purpose, isn't to be constantly stressed, struggling, or in pain.

Many miss their calling because they purposefully seek unnecessary hardship. And many avoid their calling because they think it only leads to hardship.

Sure, some stress is good. However, it is not necessary to place even more burden on ourselves. For example, exercise can provide a healthy amount of stress on the body that leads to improved health and performance. But too much stress, like lifting too much weight, or stress in the wrong areas, like hyperextending a limb, can break and even kill someone.

Not creating boundaries in response to one's natural limitations is a recipe for disaster. When we don't create healthy boundaries, we are at risk of experiencing burnout.

Many pastors encounter the backlash of burnout. They may have team members who are overcommitting to multiple responsibilities or staff that are spreading themselves too thin. What the church is left with are team members who perform mediocre work and a staff that is exhausted. Burnout in ministry poses a real threat to one's calling as well as performance.

But there are even greater threats that can come from burnout, which is more dangerous than simply poor work performance.

In my freshman year in college, there was a girl who lived on the same floor as I did. While everyone was hanging out after classes and socializing with their neighbors, she was in her dorm or in the library, working. She would be up late hours and wake up early mornings. She thought this is what college was all about. She thought that college meant studying so diligently that everything else came second to schoolwork, even her own health.

One night, she wasn't feeling too well. She wanted to email her professors for an extension on some assignments but never asked. So she spent several all-nighters in the library, fell asleep, and never woke up again. She worked her mind and body to the breaking point and, due to some health complications, died from overexhaustion.

Her parents flew to the school that same week, went into their daughter's dorm room, and permanently removed all her belongings, knowing that she would never use them again.

This girl thought that the school and her parents wanted her to be the hardest worker, but I'm sure what they would truly want is for her to still be alive.

Even though the place God is leading us toward will lead to perfection, it doesn't mean we won't face difficulties.

Even though we will have hard times on the path that God is leading us through, it doesn't mean the end goal is suffering.

Biblical Examples of Big Rock #3

"For I know the plans I have for you," declares the LORD, "plans to prosper you and not to harm you, plans to give you hope and a future."

—JEREMIAH 29:11 NIV

God spoke those words to Jeremiah so that he could share them with Israel. At this point in the Bible, the Israelites were not on good terms with God. God wasn't saying He would bring prosperity, hope, and a future to the Israelites because they deserved it. In fact, they had been breaking their covenant with God for a while. They were worshipping Canaanite Gods, sacrificing their own children, and allowing raging social injustice to happen in the land. God had told Jeremiah about how the nation would be exiled and His temple destroyed. But God also emphasized to Jeremiah that His plan wasn't to destroy the nation. God wants His people to prosper and wants them to be able to obey Him.

All the hardship and struggles that came upon the nation of Israel was a result of their disobedience and rejection of God. The same can be said for a majority of the problems everyone faces in the Bible. Time and time again, we read that God is working to transform the hearts of His people so that they will be able to keep His commandments (Deuteronomy 30:6, 10, 17–18 and Jeremiah 31:31–33).

Even the book of Revelation talks about how God plans to eliminate all suffering (Revelation 21:4).

In our still broken world, we will face struggles. But this does not mean the life God calls us toward is suffering.

To be in ministry with the mentality that work should be painful is dangerous. It can lead someone down a path where God is not calling them. This person will end up in a job that they do not enjoy, doing work they are not passionate about and becoming overly stressed because the hard work isn't meeting deeper fulfillment.

What's most unfortunate is that while a person is filling a position that leaves them unfulfilled and stressed, they are robbing someone else of the opportunity to fill the role, someone who would gladly and passionately do the work because God designed them to do it well.

A person who believes the work they do brings life to the world and brings life to themselves will produce drastically better and longer-lasting results than someone going into work with the mentality that it should be painful.

If God did not want us to enjoy the work that we do, then Adam and Eve wouldn't have been made in Eden, which in Hebrew means "Pleasure." Adam and Eve were literally working with God in Pleasure.

If God didn't want us to enjoy the work we do, then Jesus wouldn't have offered us rest for our soul and a yoke that was light and easy fitting.

If God didn't want us to enjoy life, then Jesus wouldn't have told us countless times to not be anxious.

The authors of the Bible were aware that we will face troubles, suffering, and challenges. It would be delusional to think that it is possible to avoid any struggles. Challenges and troubles are merely part of the journey that leads to greater joy, peace, and growth. To face challenges while we are pursuing our calling is to face situations that are preparing us to be able to embrace the life God is leading us toward.

It's true that not all stress should be avoided, but it's crucial to understand that not all stress is necessary.

I have told you these things, so that in me you may have peace. In this world you will have trouble. But take heart! I have overcome the world.

—JOHN 16:33 NIV

REFLECTION QUESTIONS

Answer these questions about how your buried barriers might be creating hesitation to step into your calling:

- How do I view suffering and its effect on my call to follow Jesus?

- How might always avoiding stress, or taking on too much stress, sabotage future growth in my life?

- Which biblical example stood out to you the most? What about this example caused it to stand out?

DAY 13

BONUS BARRIER: PURPOSE AND JOY IN LIFE COMES FROM THE APPROVAL OF OTHERS.

Often the fear of being ridiculed or belittled is exactly why we try to seek other's approval. This is a rock that we've all encountered and stumbled on.

When we seek approval from others, we are setting ourselves up for trouble. People's approval is wavery and can often be inconsistent. People can be very biased with how and when they give out praise or approval.

Someone can praise you when they feel particularly confident in themselves. But once you do good in an area that they feel threatens their own self-worth or identity, then you'll begin to see their true colors.

Some may be quick to encourage those who they think are below them. But when they perceive someone as ahead of themselves, they are hesitant to say anything more.

In the Bible, there are many occasions when people spitefully intend to prevent others from succeeding. Those who aren't fully embracing God's call in their life will try to bring down the lives of those who are embracing God's calling.

We read about this happening in Genesis with a young man named Joseph. Chapter 37 talks about how his stepbrothers hated him and were jealous of him. Joseph's family belittles him for the vision he has, and they try to make him feel bad about the things that God gave him. Eventually, the hatred and jealousy in the stepbrothers grew so much toward Joseph that they plotted to kill him just so they wouldn't have to bother with him or his dreams.

But Joseph wasn't the only one with family struggles. In 1 Samuel 16, we start to read about a boy named David. He was the youngest and most likely the least physically fit one in the family. Not only do his brothers criticize him, but his father doesn't even think highly of David. When you read chapter 16, David's father, Jesse, has just been informed that one of his sons is going to become king. Jesse brings in all his sons so that the prophet Samuel can discern which son will become king, but Jesse neglects to bring in one son: David. Jesse had thought so lowly of David that he had automatically assumed David couldn't possibly be king and decided to exclude him from even having the chance of being chosen.

And when it comes to being ridiculed, belittled, and threatened, Nehemiah's story exemplifies all of that. The book of Nehemiah in the Bible talks about Nehemiah's journey to build up the dilapidated city of Jerusalem. His story is full of encounters with people who are genuinely angry at him for working to rebuild Jerusalem and its broken-down walls. These people call him names. They critique his work ethic. They plot to hurt him, and when they find out that they can't hurt him, they try to simply distract him from his work. When that too fails, they resort to spreading rumors to the surrounding nations, telling them Nehemiah and the rest of the people in Jerusalem are trying to rebel.

When it comes to doing the work that God is calling us toward, we are to focus on Him, not on others.

All of those who were being oppressed and ridiculed were simply obeying God. Some of the oppressors were foreigners, and some of the oppressors were family. When reading these stories, it is easy to see who was for and who was against those that are following God's will.

But it's not the people who are clearly against us that are dangerous. Rather, it is the people who genuinely care for our well-being but don't understand the vision God has given us.

Recall the time the Israelites listened to the ten men who said they couldn't defeat the giants in the Promised Land. These men didn't want to proceed because they truly thought they couldn't beat the giants. They ended up missing out on the great blessings that God had ready for them in that land.

Recall when Saul gave David his own armor that didn't fit him. Saul thought that it was going to help protect David while fighting Goliath. Little did Saul know that all David needed was a sling and some smooth stones.

Recall Peter telling Jesus that he wouldn't allow the government to kill him. Peter wanted the best for Jesus and saw Jesus's death as a bad thing. Little did he know that Jesus's death would lead to eternal life.

Just remember:

- The world doesn't want us to live up to our potential—Joseph and his brothers (Genesis 37:2-10, 18-20)

- The world will see our intrinsic worth as being based on extrinsic ranking—David being the youngest (1 Samuel 16:1-13)

- The world wants us to adopt a story that is not our own—Gideon in the weakest clan (Judges 6:14-16)

- The world will have us doubt who God made us to be—Jesus having his identity challenged by the devil (Matthew 4:1-11)

REFLECTION QUESTIONS

Answer these questions about how your buried barriers might be creating hesitation to step into your calling:

- When do I derive my purpose and joy from the approval of others?

- How does seeking the approval or praise of others diminish the growth in my life?

- Which biblical example stood out to you the most? What about this example caused it to stand out?

LET'S DIG EXERCISE! REFLECTING ON FALSE FOUNDATIONAL BELIEFS

These rocks will not be easy to dig up. The bigger they are and the deeper they're buried, the more time and effort is required to remove them.

Having the background knowledge and awareness of these barriers is the first step to removing them. The second step is to take time prayerfully bringing them to God and carefully exposing each one.

Just play with the idea that you may have at least one rock that's a barrier.

Each one will prevent you from reaching newer depths and greater growth spiritually, relationally, and vocationally.

Like a root that is trying to grow deep in soil, if there is a large, dense rock in the way, the root can't go any deeper, and the plant can't grow any larger. The same is true for your life and ministry.

Answer these questions to summarize what you learned in this chapter:

- Which barrier resonated with you the most in your current season?

- How has this barrier negatively impacted growth?

- Imagine if, one year from now, you had no hesitation in pursuing God's call on your life. What would your life look like? How might you feel?

DIGGING WRAP-UP

At this point, since you have gone through the cultivating section and the digging section, I'm sure some memories of things in the past have come to mind that may not be comfortable to think about.

But what I want you to know is that every garden that grows the biggest fruits the fastest has the most manure in the soil! There's a lot of crap that is required to properly fertilize a garden. God has designed the world in a way where the crap we have can become the nutrient-rich resource that infuses our soil with exactly the right stuff that a fruitful life needs.

Joseph's entire story is about people putting him through a lot of crap, but in the end, he was able to confidently say...

You intended to harm me, but God intended it for good to accomplish what is now being done, the saving of many lives.
— GENESIS 50:20 NIV

God accounts for tragedies and can accomplish great things through you despite all the crap that might have been, or currently is, going on in your life.

So don't let crappy memories become unnecessary burdens when God intends to use them to produce great fruit in your life. I don't want to minimize the events of your past. I merely want to encourage you to not give them any more power or weight than they already have in your life.

Chapter 4

ENVISIONING

DAY 14: IMAGINE THE ENDGAME

Take a moment to appreciate how far you have come on this journey.

You are doing something that others won't take the time and energy to invest in. You are committing to understand and mature more, which is something that most are not willing to do.

You're on your way to creating not only more fruitfulness in your life but also more fulfillment. To be at this point in the book means that you are willing to take your life to that next level of growth and impact. God is working in you and around you to bring clarity and massive transformation.

This section will be focusing specifically on clarity.

Without any clarity, we can find ourselves waiting for apples under a tree that bares no fruit. Or moving in a direction that brings us to the wrong destination. Or making sacrifices in order to be satisfied, only to discover we've been sacrificing the very things that would bring satisfaction.

That is exactly what this section will help you to prevent. It seems simple, but many of us forget to envision what our end-game is.

Before we start planting a garden, we need to envision what the garden will become. How do we want this garden to be managed? What foliage or vegetation should be used? And where should everything be planted?

A simple plan with some simple prayer and meditation can help to provide us with a grander and broader perspective that will allow us to envision our calling.

DON'T DISCOUNT YOUR LIFE

The ground of a certain rich man yielded an abundant harvest. He thought to himself, "What shall I do? I have no place to store my crops." Then he said, "This is what I'll do. I will tear down my barns and build bigger ones, and there I will store my surplus grain. And I'll say to myself, 'You have plenty of grain laid up for many years. Take life easy; eat, drink and be merry.'" But God said to him, "You fool! This very night your life will be demanded from you. Then who will get what you have prepared for yourself?" This is how it will be with whoever stores up things for themselves but is not rich toward God.

—LUKE 12:16–21 NIV

This parable gave us a glimpse into what can happen when our whole life is lived with a narrow perspective and misplaced priorities. The rich man, who is so focused on multiplying his income and improving his business, had not thought about where all his hard work and accomplishments would bring him. He sacrificed so much of his time in growing his income that he neglected to grow his relationships with his friends and family, hence not knowing who will get what he prepared for himself. He probably sacrificed so much joy and peace in the hopes of one day being able to relax. When he was told his life would end, I'm sure he looked at all he had worked so hard to earn and saw it as worthless.

Clearly, the rich man had misplaced values because he had a short-term perspective. But this type of behavior isn't abnormal.

Nir Eyal, an expert in the field of behavior engineering and *Wall Street Journal* best-selling author of *Hooked*, says that human beings have a natural bias toward "Hyperbolic Discounting." This is when we opt for smaller, immediate rewards, such as having more money rather than waiting for greater benefits that may take longer to accrue, like growing deeper relationships.

Scientific studies have shown that if people are offered to take $100 now or $105 in 1 week, statistically, people are more likely to choose the $100 now. However, if this same group were asked if they would rather receive $100 in a year or $105 in a year and one week, then they are more likely to opt for the $105. The rationale behind waiting a year and one week is, "I'll already be waiting a year. Might as well wait one more week."

What's fascinating is, whether a person is waiting a week or a year and one week, that extra week is worth five dollars in both scenarios. Only when the group was asked to view the scenario in a long-term perspective were they able to see the value of waiting that extra week.

Since hyperbolic discounting can cause us to act or behave in a way that is not beneficial or wise in the long term, we need to be extra careful to avoid making decisions based solely on immediate reward.

A perfect example of this is when Judas betrays Jesus. Judas sacrifices someone who was not only a teacher to him but was also a friend and messiah in his eyes. Why did Judas betray Jesus? Judas saw thirty pieces of silver as a greater reward than what Jesus was offering him. Judas wanted to make a little extra money now, instead of waiting to earn greater riches in heaven.

When our sights are focused only on what is in front of us, we can miss out on the big picture.

King Saul didn't wait for Samuel to perform the necessary sacrifice before going to war. Why? He doubted that Samuel was going to show up to perform the sacrifice, and he didn't want to wait any longer. Saul disobeyed a clear command that was given to him prior to this moment in the story, and it resulted in Saul losing his dominion over Israel. At that moment, Saul saw it too costly to wait any longer and chose to immediately perform the animal sacrifice and jump right into battle.

In the parable of the rich man, the rich man saw the short-term cost of amassing a huge harvest as more valuable than building thriving, long-lasting relationships with God and others. The short-term gain of more money was perceived as being greater than the effort required to grow rich toward God. What's sad is that the rich man sacrificed his relationships to get more wealth only to die without having time to enjoy all that he had amassed and not having anyone to enjoy the riches with. He could have had thriving relationships, a comfortable amount of income, and been able to enjoy his whole life instead of discounting it.

Only when the rich man was forced to view his life in the big picture did he see the short-term gain was not worth the long-term sacrifice.

Another theory as to why the rich man behaved the way he did is due to something called "transactional utility." Richard Thaler—a Nobel Memorial Prize winner in economic sciences and professor of behavioral science and economics at the University of Chicago Booth School of Business—mentions this term in his book *Misbehaving: The Making of Behavioral Economics*.

Thaler describes transactional utility as the happiness a consumer gets from the perceived value of a deal. Whether or not there is a good deal is irrelevant. In Thaler's studies, he noticed that if there is a greater perception of a deal, then someone is more likely to make decisions in favor of the deal rather than the actual value it provides.

For example, let's say a consumer is looking to buy a thirty-dollar pair of shoes. Before purchasing the shoes, they learn that if they walk fifteen minutes to a store up the street, they could get the same shoes at 20 percent off, which is a savings of six dollars. There is a high probability that the consumer would walk fifteen minutes in order to save the six dollars.

Now let's say the same consumer is looking to buy shoes worth $300. They learn that if they walk fifteen minutes to a store up the street, they could get the same shoes at 2 percent off, which is also a savings of six dollars. Even though the fifteen-minute walk could save them six dollars, as in scenario one, the consumer is statistically less likely to make the same walk.

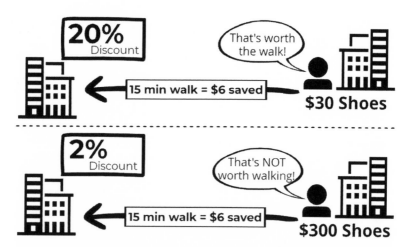

Despite saving the same amount in both scenarios, the rationale for making the fifteen-minute walk in scenario one but not in scenario two is that 20 percent off is a greater deal than 2 percent off.

If walking fifteen minutes is worth the effort of saving six dollars, it shouldn't matter if it is a 20 percent discount or a 2 percent discount. But that is the effect of transactional utility.

If you don't want to find yourself discounting your life, you need to understand:

1. What the true value is

2. The cost associated with our choice

If you can recognize the true cost and value, then you are setting yourself up for making wiser, more fruitful decisions.

There are many instances in the Bible in which people discount their life. We read about this happening in Genesis 25:29–34 when Esau sells his birthright to Jacob in order to get some red stew.

Esau's attention was on his stomach. The hunger pangs were his immediate focus. His rationale was that his birthright was intangible and not beneficial to him in that instant. If he wanted the benefits of his birthright, he would need to wait. But he didn't want to wait. He was hungry now and wanted to eat now, not later.

Neglecting to see the value of his birthright and the cost of giving it up, Esau concluded giving an intangible birthright in exchange for something immediately tangible was a greater deal!

But Jacob was smart. Jacob understood the true value of Esau's birthright. Jacob knew the cost of exchanging food for a birthright was worth every last drop of red stew he had.

What hyperbolic discounting and transactional utility teach us is that if our sights are set too narrow, if our values are not properly aligned, and the cost of our actions aren't accounted for, then we may reach the end of our lives and realize we had sacrificed the very thing that would give us what we need. And no one wants to be like the rich man in the parable, Judas when Jesus was crucified, Saul when he lost his rulership, or Esau when he had no birthright.

We often fail to view the world and our lives in a larger perspective. Sometimes we forget to recognize where we are deriving the measures by which we value our life. You may be fortunate enough to not have lost something like rulership over a kingdom or encountered something as drastic as getting someone you loved killed. But we have all, at one point in our lives, chosen immediate gratification or fallen victim to the perceived deal instead of waiting for greater fulfillment and choosing the better investment.

Rarely do we take the time to step back and ask:

- "Are the things that I am sacrificing now leading me to become the person who God has made me to be?"

- "If my life were to end right now, can I confidently say I had lived it to the fullest?"

- "Is my behavior reflecting how I want others to remember me?"

Questions like these can help us to break out of the habit of hyperbolic discounting and transactional utility. Envisioning our life from a greater perspective helps to reorient our heart and refocus our sights on what's truly valuable.

Like a muscle, meditating on things that have us imagine beyond just ourselves and our current situation, can make it easier to *"fix our eyes not on what is seen, but on what is unseen, since what is seen is temporary, but what is unseen is eternal"* (2 Corinthians 4:18 NIV).

By envisioning our life in the big picture and seeing the endgame, we are stretching our imagination. Our heart begins to yearn for more purpose beyond just the material or momentary. We begin to ask ourselves if how we are reacting, what we are sacrificing, and where we are going, is helping us become the person God is leading you and me to be.

Sure, it may be easy to try and visualize how your life may look or feel by the end of today, the end of this book, or even the end of this year. But let's take it further than that and picture what our life will look like when our life here on earth is over.

DAY 15: THE ENDGAME

Before there was the Apostle Paul, there was the Pharisee Saul. Growing up as a Jewish boy in Tarsus, Saul went on to study under the great Rabbi Gamaliel. Eventually, Saul was employed by the high priest to hunt down the Jewish men, women, and children who started following a strange teacher named Jesus.

On the surface, Saul thought he was being driven by the right values. He thought he was heading in the right direction and doing the right thing. But when he was forced to view his life in the grand scheme of God's purpose for him, his whole identity and perspective changed.

When Saul was on his way to Damascus to attack even more Christians, he was blinded by the light that came from heaven. He then encountered Jesus, who asked him, *"'Saul, Saul, why do you persecute me?' And Saul said, 'Who are you, Lord?' And Jesus said, 'I am Jesus, whom you are persecuting.'"* (Acts 9:4–5).

For three days, Saul could not physically see. Yet he saw that he wasn't being led by the right ideas or the right values. By losing his sight, he was forced to stop looking at what was immediately in front of him. He began to focus on what God wanted him to see. For three days, Saul chose to not eat or drink so that he could gain more clarity and revelation from God as to what was happening to him.

Saul, the man who was killing Christians, became Paul, God's chosen instrument, who carried Jesus's name to Gentiles, kings, and children of Israel.

Paul went from trying to destroy Christianity to then encouraging and building up the very people whom he had been persecuting. But this dramatic shift in his career and dramatic transformation of his identity only happened when Saul:

- Encountered Jesus and reflected on why he was working so diligently to persecute him (Acts 9:3–5).

- Was forced to refocus on the big picture of his life (Acts 9:9).

- Was shown a vision by Jesus (Act 9:16).

After all of this, Paul could now see the big picture. He knew what his life's purpose was and how he would step into that role. Although he knew this journey would be full of suffering, he also knew it would be more fulfilling and more meaningful than anything the world had to offer.

We too can have transformation like Paul. We too can lead a meaningful, purposeful, and impactful life like Paul did through the ministry Jesus gave him.

Some of the factors that led to Paul living out a life and ministry that brought fulfillment and long-lasting change started with:

1. Looking to heaven

2. Recognizing the condition of his garden

3. Seeing what God wanted to plant in his life

Paul had a clear understanding of his destination and the outcome. Paul could see the endgame.

Knowing the endgame is like knowing where a target is. A target that is out of focus is a target that can't be hit, and if we know where we are aiming, we can better hit the mark.

This is true in many areas of life. For example, before there is a business, there is a business plan to define where the company is going and what its employees will need to prioritize.

Before there is a building, there are blueprints to help the builders know how to make the foundation and create the structures to support the building.

Before going on a road trip, a road map shows where you're going and how to get to the destination. It helps to keep the traveler on track and can show how close or how far away they are to the destination.

Visualizing the endgame helps to:

- Define the outcome

- Refine the purpose

- Determine the values that'll draw us toward the outcome

Without an endgame, we will be like Saul: someone who works hard but for the wrong reasons. Someone who gets far, but in the wrong direction. Someone who is rich, but not rich toward God.

But when we understand the endgame, we become like Paul. Someone who understands their priorities, values, direction, and purpose.

IMAGINING THE ENDGAME EXERCISE

This day I call the heavens and the earth as witnesses against you that I have set before you life and death, blessings and curses. Now choose life, so that you and your children may live.

—DEUTERONOMY 30:19 NIV

The verse above came at a point in Moses's career when he knew his time of leadership, and life, was over. After failing to bring the nation of Israel into the Promised Land, Moses had to give the next generation something that would lead them in the right direction. Moses knew the current condition of the people's heart. The nation knew where they were going. The paths were clear, and Moses made the options simple. Choose life or death.

It seems dramatic, but if the road to life is not taken, then it's clear that any other road is one that leads away from life. The same can be said for our own journey.

Is what we are doing, what we are saying, or how we are reacting helping us to become the person God is leading us to be or not?

To know whether we are stepping into the Promised Land or away from it, we first need to know where it is that God wants to lead us.

As you proceed, really take the time to write out what you are feeling and thinking. Don't rush, and don't feel pressured to write things out perfectly. We're merely prayerfully imagining.

This section is just the envisioning portion. The actual structuring and forming of your calling comes later.

As you go, follow the steps, and try to be in an area where you won't be easily distracted. Allow yourself time to answer the questions to the best of your ability.

If you find yourself running out of space to write your notes in this book, feel free to use a separate piece of paper to write your responses.

Step 1: Write down three people who you deeply respect relationally, vocationally, and spiritually. It doesn't matter if they are alive or deceased, a close friend or someone you had never met. Just put down one person you admire respectively for each area.

- Someone who leads their family well:

    ○

    ○

    ○

- Someone who leads well in their vocation:

    ○

    ○

    ○

- Someone whom you admire that is more mature spiritually:

    ○

    ○

    ○

After you write down the three people you respect in each category, list three qualities you admire most for each person.

Step 2: How would you describe who you are relationally, vocationally, and spiritually when you're at your best?

Step 3: Imagine you are encountering your older self. What would the three most important lessons be that the older version of you would tell the current you?

Once you have written your response, answer this question: Why are those lessons so important?

Step 4: Imagine there is a room full of people whom you hold close to your heart. Family members whom you love, friends whom you care deeply for, and others whom you admire are all in this room. At the front of the room, there is a podium. One by one, those who you love and are close with begin to line up by the podium. They are getting ready to speak, and you begin to realize that they are all getting ready to speak at your funeral.

Who at your funeral is lining up to share about your life? The list of people can be as long or as short as you want. Just be sure these are all people whom you hold close to your heart. Write those from your

- Immediate Family (Parents, siblings, spouse, children, extended relatives)

- Friend group

- Work environment/profession

- Church or organization where you volunteer

Step 5: What difference would you like to have made in each person's life?

Step 6: What kind of character would you like them to have seen in you?

Step 7: To wrap up our exercises of looking at your life from a larger perspective, now it's time to get laser focused on the present to understand why it is that you do what you do. The exercise we will go through is one that I learned from Dean Graziosi called the Seven Levels Deep Exercise. This exercise will uncover your deeper *why*. It's the reason why you push through difficulties, take steps of faith, and move forward when others have given up.

Although some of the questions may seem repetitive in this last step, each serve a purpose to reveal what deeply inspires and drives you. Each question you answer will bring you into a deeper level of understanding what's at the center of your heart.

You'll start by writing down what you believe is the main goal you want to achieve in your life.

*Main Goal:*_____

    A. Why is it important to you that you achieve that goal?

    B. Why is it important that you [answer from a]?

    C. Why is it important that you [answer from b]?

D. Why is it important that you [answer from c]?

E. Why is it important that you [answer from d]?

F. Why is it important that you [answer from e]?

G. Why is it important that you [answer from f]?

By reaching and answering question G, what you are left with is your true why. It's the essence of why you are seeking your calling and purpose. It's why you get out of bed in the morning. It's why you are going on this journey. And it's why you have gotten this far in *Planting Your Purpose*.

ENDGAME WRAP-UP

A good reputation is better than precious perfume; likewise, the day of one's death is better than the day of one's birth.

—ECCLESIASTES 7:1 NIV

By going through and thoroughly answering these questions, you started the process of visualizing the endgame. What you wrote were the beginning steps toward describing the fundamental values that can inspire and influence the trajectory of your growth. Notice how your writing is more than just gaining, reaching, or achieving. At its core, life is about giving.

At funerals, people don't talk about the value of a life based on how much the individual *gained*. Rather, it's about how much the individual *gave* and who they *became*.

We see that the success we are defining is based on contributing, not simply accomplishing.

As you discover and clearly define the person whom God is calling you to be, you can more easily:

- Gauge how closely your daily actions reflect who God is making you to be.

- Track if your daily actions are contributing meaningfully to the vision and mission you have for your life.

- Avoid the trap of being busy without being effective.

With the endgame in mind, you'll have a clearer vision of how your flourishing garden is going to look. You'll have a better idea of what we should plant in our garden.

Chapter 5

PLANTING

DAY 16: PLANTING PURPOSE

I'm very excited to be speaking with you at this point in the journey. You are in a league that is far beyond where many have been before. Rarely do I encounter someone who is as determined and persistent as you are.

Take time to appreciate all that you have learned and discovered up until this point. Soon, you will have all the materials you need in order to define the fruitful calling God has for you.

We worked to remove false values and ideas from our hearts (cultivating). This helped to create a more fertile environment for good values to thrive!

We then began to identify and remove the deeply buried beliefs that may have been hindering greater growth from already happening in our lives (digging).

By visualizing the endgame and reflecting on what drives us, we started to imagine what a fruitful life could consist of. This also started the brainstorming process, which will help us pinpoint the good values that we might most deeply identify with.

Now, it's time to find the values that God wants to plant in our garden.

We'll be combining the imaginative and conscious part of our self-awareness to craft an empowering and impactful vision and mission. One that is built on values that Jesus teaches, which will deeply penetrate our hearts, inspire us to live with integrity, and bring fruitfulness in our lives and ministry. This section is dedicated to helping you write out an effective vision and mission that can develop and guide you in being the person God is calling you to be.

LET'S PLANT!

Try not to become a man of success, but rather try to become a man of value.

—ALBERT EINSTEIN

A personal vision and mission statement shouldn't be underestimated. Creating one based on deeply rooted values and correct principles can be the basis for discerning daily habits, direction, and decisions that bring fruitfulness and fulfillment.

Having an effective vision and mission statement is more than just picking good values and using proper grammar. The most effective and long-lasting statements are ones that use values which we deeply identify with.

Defining our findings and refining them into a statement won't happen overnight. The most effective and empowering statements require careful analysis, deep reflection, and many rewrites.

Even after completing a statement that you feel comfortable with, you'll need to review it regularly and ask yourself, "Does my statement require any minor adjustments now that I have additional insights/changes in and around me?"

This journey has not been about inventing something new. We've simply been discovering what God had already planned for us.

At its core, your vision and mission will always be an expression of your deepest values found in Jesus.

When you take the time to review and reflect on the values and lifestyle of Jesus, you are consciously trying to align your beliefs and behavior with that of Jesus's.

So, let's go from theory to action as we clarify our statement in writing.

Step 1: Understanding the Journey

Vision and mission communicates your calling and allows purpose to grow in your life. A compelling vision and mission consist of more than just an amalgamation of fancy words and memorable phrases. It stems from an understanding of *how* and *why* these statements deeply resonate with you.

This first step in understanding the how and why is to understand the journey.

Throughout this whole book, we have been working to recognize where you are and where God is leading you. These two things, knowing where you are and where you are going, are the backbone of any journey.

But what matters most isn't getting to the destination; it's about who you become by the end of it.

On Jesus's journey in ministry, He faced countless trials that challenged His character and attempted to deviate Him from the path that God was leading Him on.

On our journey, we can also expect to face challenges that will tempt us to break integrity and go down the wrong path. To prepare for this and overcome these hurdles, we will use the notes and knowledge learned throughout this book to form a summary of your journey.

This summary will be comprised of statements and beliefs about who you are and how you live. Knowing who you are will help to fight back any doubts about who God made you to be. Knowing how you live will help you to walk with integrity and remain on the right path.

This summary you create is going to feel:

- Ambitious and realistic

- Lofty yet specific

- Overreaching but still personal

When crafting this summary, feel free to lean more toward making it admirable and bold. Often, it's the unusually ambitious journeys that bring about a greater perspective, a greater purpose, and greater reliance on God.

A journey that simply reflects the person you already are, or can easily be, will lead to a vision and mission that is dull and uninspiring. An average-sounding journey leads to average effort and mediocre results. It's been said, "If a vision is from God, then it will require you to rely on and have faith in God. If you have a vision that you can easily do alone, then it's not a vision from God."

Your summary of your journey may be as simple as stringing together all your notes into a short paragraph. Ideally, you want to get your summary written out in as few sentences as possible. The fewer the sentences, the more powerful, meaningful, and impactful it'll be.

Action

1. Review your notes from each chapter and highlight or star the notes that you find are the most important.

2. Using the space provided, summarize the notes for each chapter respectively. Try to write it in three to five sentences. As you summarize the notes, phrase them in a way that makes it personal and promotes you to take a positive action! (For example, let's say you have a note from the "Envisioning" section that says, "It's crucial to do the important tasks." You could rephrase this to say, "*I will do* the important tasks *first*." Now it is both personal and promotes positive action!)

    A. Cultivating notes

    B. Digging notes

    C. Envisioning notes

3. Combine the summarized notes you wrote for question two into a single, unified paragraph. Feel free to play with the order of your notes. You can write them in a way that creates a flow and structure that best resonates for you!

DAY 17

Step 2: Which seeds will you plant?

In Genesis, we read about a boy named Joseph. As a child, Joseph received a vision from God, showing him that he would gain great authority in the future. Throughout Joseph's journey, God gave him many opportunities to trust in Him and respond to hardship in a way that reflected the characteristics of a good and responsible leader.

Joseph's integrity was tested every moment of his young adult life. He followed a code of conduct that he believed allowed him to live a life that would honor God and those around him. Every test allowed Joseph to courageously trust God and exemplify Godly characteristics.

But it wouldn't have been possible for Joseph to keep integrity if he lacked the forethought to know what his values were.

Picking and planting values into your vision and mission requires being aware of and connecting with the deeply held values that God has placed in you.

These will be the seeds that sprout our enduring code of conduct, the rules of engagement that we follow while on this journey of living out our calling.

You not only want to make sure you are picking the values that you best identify with, but you also want to make sure you are picking values that are good.

Whatever you plant, or neglect to plant, will influence your:

- Identity: Your sense of self-worth, emotional intelligence, and integrity.

- Trajectory: Your sense of direction in life and the principles you abide by.

- Discernment: Wisdom used for decision-making, understanding, and judging situations.

- Strength and Endurance: The ability to act righteously, step out courageously, and have the capacity to keep doing good work.

You will always harvest what you plant. Those who live only to satisfy their own sinful nature will harvest decay and death from that sinful nature. But those who live to please the Spirit will harvest everlasting life from the Spirit. So, let's not get tired of doing what is good. At just the right time we will reap a harvest of blessing if we don't give up. Therefore, whenever we have the opportunity, we should do good to everyone—especially to those in the family of faith.

—GALATIANS 6:7–10

Knowing and having the right seeds to plant can be the difference between having a flourishing garden or a thicket of mangled vegetation. Planting the right seeds will allow your identity, trajectory, discernment, strength, and endurance to blossom!

With greater identity, you develop a clearer trajectory.

The clearer your trajectory, the better your discernment.

And being able to properly discern situations will allow you to build strength and endurance in the right way. Thus, getting you closer and closer to living out your purpose.

Things to keep in mind moving forward:

- You're unique. Therefore, your statement style and content should embrace this. Don't be afraid to deviate from the provided examples or layout, and don't merely copy them.

- The values should acknowledge your character and contributions. Think, "Who do I want to be?" and "What do I want to contribute?" and "How are my values reflected by my character?"

On the next page is a list of values that can be found when studying Jesus's life in ministry. Be sure to refer to the notes you've been taking throughout this book while you peruse the list. Pick values that line up with your summarized journey from "Step 1: Understanding the Journey." This will help to refine which values you most deeply identify with. Also, if you find that the synonyms for the values provided can better express the word's meaning and application to your daily life, you are welcomed to use synonyms instead.

Action: Referring to your summarized journey from earlier, circle which values best express your journey. The values you choose should inspire you and bring about a sense of internal satisfaction and excitement.

The goal isn't to try and cram the most values into a single statement. Rather, it's to define which values penetrate the deepest in your heart.

Try to pick the few, most impactful values that resonate with you. Keep in mind, the more values you pick, the more work you will have to do later.

AUTHENTICITY	FRIENDSHIPS	LEADERSHIP
ADVENTURE	FUN	LEARNING
BALANCE	GENEROSITY	LOVE
BOLDNESS	GENTLENESS	LOYALTY
COMPASSION	GENUINENESS	OPENNESS
COMMITMENT	GOODNESS	OPTIMISM
COMMUNITY	GRATITUDE	PATIENCE
COMPETENCY	GROWTH	PEACE
COURAGE	HAPPINESS	POISE
CREATIVITY	HEALTH	PERSEVERANCE
CURIOSITY	HONESTY	RESPECT
DETERMINATION	HUMILITY	RESPONSIBILITY
EMPATHY	HUMOR	SECURITY
ENCOURAGEMENT	HARMONY	SELF-CONTROL
EXCELLENCE	INTEGRITY	SELF-RESPECT
FAIRNESS	JOY	SERVANT
FAITHFULNESS	JUSTICE	STABILITY
FORGIVENESS	KINDNESS	SYMPATHY
FREEDOM	KNOWLEDGE	TRUSTWORTHINESS
		WISDOM

DAY 18

Step 3: Crafting Values into Virtues

Now that you have selected your values, we are going to write out how we intend to live out these values as virtues. Virtues define how we aim to embody the values in our daily life, shifting from belief to behavior.

For example, we may believe respect for others is an important value. Its virtue could be, "I will respect others by listening and understanding their perspective first before contributing my own opinions," or "I demonstrate respect for others by investing time and resources into developing those around me."

However, a virtue isn't an action that is performed during rare or specific occasions. An example of this would be, "Respect Aunt Laurel by waiting at least sixty seconds before contributing my thoughts."

That is not a virtue because it isn't a statement that can be applied to daily life, and it is written as a rule rather than a way of living.

Action: Turn your values into virtues by following these prompts. Make sure your answers are specific enough to be intentionally done but vague enough as to not be a onetime occurrence.

1. Pick one of the values you selected from "Step 2: Which Seeds Will You Plant?" to answer these questions respectively.

2. What does it look like to act on this value in your daily life?

3. What positive impact would this produce in your:

   A. Life

   B. Ministry/vocation

   C. Relationships

4. Now, use another value you have selected from "Step 2: Which Seeds Will You Plant?" to answer the questions. Repeat until you use all your values. If you find yourself running out of space to write your notes in this book, feel free to use a separate piece of paper to write your responses.

DAY 19

Step 4: Planting Purpose

Having values and virtues is nothing unless it is incorporated into our daily life. It would be like having seeds and never planting them. Seeds that aren't planted can't produce any fruit.

So now that we have our virtues, let's integrate them into the various crucial roles you have in life. You may be an entrepreneur, parent, sibling, husband, wife, friend, or mentor, all of which have various responsibilities and commitments associated with them. Identifying the various roles in your life and anticipating how you plan to live out the virtues defined earlier will help to create better balance and harmony as you begin to live out your vision and mission.

Being too overly absorbed by the external demands of one role can have us forget the overall direction that God is leading us. Having our roles written out in front of us allows us to frequently review and reorient where we are facing.

Think of how easy it could have been for David to forget his role and values while being hunted down by King Saul. David had many opportunities to kill Saul, but David knew that in doing so, it would have gone against his character and gone against God's will.

God had Samuel anoint Saul to be king over Israel (1 Samuel 10:1), and even though David had been anointed at a young age to replace King Saul (1 Samuel 16:13), David's faith in God compelled him to wait. David trusted God and was content to wait on God's timing for when Saul should no longer be king.

If David were to have killed Saul, David would have been known as the first person in Israel's history to have killed one of its kings. Not only that, but Saul was David's father-in-law and the father of his best friend Jonathan. By killing Saul, David would have murdered the king and the father of his wife and best friend.

This is what David told Saul only moments after passing up the opportunity to kill him:

Look, my father in law, at what I have in my hand. It is a piece of the hem of your robe! I cut it off, but I didn't kill you. This proves that I am not trying to harm you and that I have not sinned against you, even though you have been hunting for me to kill me.

May the LORD judge between us. Perhaps the LORD will punish you for what you are trying to do to me, but I will never harm you. As that old proverb says, "From evil people come evil deeds." So you can be sure I will never harm you.

—1 SAMUEL 24:11–13 NLT

If David chose to kill Saul and rush into the role of being king, he would have broken his integrity, broken his trust in God, broken his relationship to his wife and Jonathan, and would have been disloyal to the king. Since David knew who he was, where he was, who God was, and where God was leading him, David was able to live out a righteous life as a young man, which exemplified his worthiness of being king.

Action: Follow these steps so that you can have a greater understanding of how to live out your virtues in the various roles you may have in life.

1. List two to three roles that you serve that are most crucial in your life.

2. For each role, answer the following questions:

    A. Which two to four values would best benefit you and those around you in this role?

    B. What does it look like to live out your virtues in this role?

    C. What positive impact would be made if you consistently lived out your virtues in this role?

DAY 20

Step 5: Writing your Vision and Mission

By this point, you should have a pretty good understanding of which values and virtues bring greater fruitfulness. We discerned which values inspire greater growth, as well as how to integrate virtues into your life.

When you form your vision and mission, it'll have more meaning because it will be attached to such deeply rooted values and virtues.

Now, let's write out the vision and mission.

You have the option to create a vision and mission for each of the roles that you wrote about in Step 4, or you can try to answer these questions and create one broad vision and mission that can be applied in all areas.

Action: Fill in the prompts.

For your vision:

1. Select one of the roles you answered in "Step 4: Planting Purpose." (For example, a role I selected was husband.)

2. Order the values you associated with that role by their level

of importance to you in that role. (For example, my values consisted of trustworthiness, generosity, servant, and encouragement.)

3. Fill in the blanks below. Keep in mind, the grammar may need to be adjusted. The values should be written as a verb or adjective. (For example, "servant" is a noun. To make it work in my vision statement, I changed it to the verb form "serving." For "trustworthiness," I used the adjective form of the word, which is "trustworthy.")

   A. To be a [verb/adjective form of the values in order of importance] [role in your life]. (Example: To be a trustworthy, encouraging, generous, and serving husband.)

For your mission:

1. Referring back to question two in "Step 3: Crafting Values into Virtues," select only the answers that match the same values in your vision statement, then write them in the same order you wrote your values in your vision statement.

2. Referring back to question three from your notes in "Step 3: Crafting Values into Virtues," write your positive impacts in the same order you wrote your values in your vision statement. Only pick the positive impacts that match the values of your vision *and* are related to the role in your vision.

    A. For example, if the role in your vision is spouse, friend, or sibling, then "relationship" is most closely related to those roles. Therefore, you would pick the responses you wrote for relationships. If, for example, the role in your vision is leader, intern, mentor, or employee, then you might select the positive impact for ministry/vocation as that is most closely related to those roles.

3. Fill in the blanks:

    A. I will [answers you used for question one in your mission]. I do this so that [answers you used for question two in your mission]

Once you complete all the steps for your vision and mission with one role, you may go back and follow the steps again with the other roles that you fulfill in life.

Here is an example of what your vision and mission may look like:

To be a trustworthy, encouraging, generous, and serving husband.

I act immediately on promises and commitments, I seek and speak light on my wife's strengths, I give and don't grumble despite feelings of lacking, and I contribute to the greater benefit of my wife. I do this so that she can have confidence in what I say, feel empowered in what she does, feel unconditionally loved, and receive a boatload of mercy and grace.

Now you have your vision and mission written out. You also have a few other useful tools, such as your credo, values, and virtues that you can use.

Reviewing the notes from this section can help to remind you of the journey you took as well as inspire you on your journey ahead.

What I recommend is to read over your vision and mission daily. Try to memorize it. I also recommend reviewing the notes of this section every chance you get. Make it into a habit. The more time you spend reading your notes and internalizing them, the more God can use it to grow you.

Even after creating a vision and mission that you feel comfortable with, you'll need to review it regularly and ask yourself, "Does my statement require any minor adjustments now that I have additional insights/changes in and around me?"

In order to help you further polish up your statement, let's go through three factors that make for a fruitful vision and mission statement!

THREE FACTORS FOR A FRUITFUL VISION AND MISSION

True greatness is not measured by the headlines a person commands or the wealth he or she accumulates. The inner character of a person— the undergirding moral and spiritual values and commitments—is the true measure of lasting greatness.

—BILLY GRAHAM

To help you structure the best statement, let's go through some of the defining factors that have been found to make the most fruitful statements. Here are the three defining factors.

Factor One: The statement should be focused on how you are giving to God and others.

If I were to tell you to imagine something that is constantly giving, always producing light, and gives structure to everything around it, what image comes to mind? If you were to say I was describing the characteristics of a godly man or woman, you wouldn't be wrong. But if you were to say I was describing the sun, you wouldn't be wrong either.

Our sun is the cornerstone to all life in our solar system. It gives out energy, heat, and light freely without needing to be fed into. It's massive and has everything it needs to produce light for the planets that orbit around it. The sun gives structure and order for us on Earth, such as holding together our solar system and allowing for time of day and seasons. The sun not only plays an important role in promoting life on Earth, it protects life too. The sun's magnetic field creates a very large protective bubble called the heliosphere, which shields the planets from harmful cosmic radiation. It encapsulates not just the Earth, but our entire solar system.

In contrast, if I were to ask you to imagine something that is dense, void of producing light, never giving, and always taking, you might imagine a family member, coworker, or troubled acquaintance. But if you were to imagine a black hole, you wouldn't be wrong.

Black holes are dense objects that only pull things in and never give anything back. Everything that gets close to them is ripped apart and destroyed. They are so dense that not even light can be reflected. A black hole doesn't snuff out or cover the light. It just pulls light in, never letting it go.

The difference between asking, "How can I contribute?" as opposed to "How can the world contribute to me?" is like the difference between our sun and a black hole.

Shifting from self to others is what brings us from having a worldly perspective to a heavenly perspective and changes worldly work to Godly work.

As you read the next few verses, notice how Jesus talks about his ministry and where his focus is. He makes it very clear that his purpose on Earth wasn't to meet his own needs and desires. At the heart of what he was doing was God's will, and it was expressed by serving others.

For even the Son of Man came not to be served but to serve others and to give his life as a ransom for many.

—MARK 10:45 NIV

For I have come down from heaven to do the will of God who sent me, not to do my own will.

—JOHN 6:38 NLT

My Father! If it is possible, let this cup of suffering be taken away from me. Yet I want your will to be done, not mine.

—MATTHEW 26:39 NLT (ALSO LUKE 22:42, MARK 14:36)

In Colossians, Paul talks about how we are to clothe ourselves in mercy, kindness, humility, gentleness, and patience, making allowances and forgiving those who offend us (Colossians 3:1–3, 12–13). But these behaviors that Paul mentioned can only happen when we are responding to situations which promote the opposite. If we are to be merciful, it means the others have messed up. If we are to be kind, it means we are to be friendly even if the other person isn't. If we are to be humble, it means we must turn away from the opportunity to be prideful. If we are to be gentle, that means we are capable of being brutal. If we are to be patient, it means we are in a situation that requires waiting.

The only way we can behave this way is if we are in the company of others and are selflessly giving to others. Therefore, a statement should be focused on giving, not gaining, and the only way we can give is if we are giving to someone else.

Factor Two: The statement should motivate you because of the intrinsic satisfaction it provides.

"Intrinsic satisfaction" is a phrase that we don't hear too often. Another way of phrasing it can be to use the word "joy." Therefore, the statement should motivate you because of the joy it provides.

The Holy Spirit produces this kind of fruit in our lives: love, joy, peace, patience, kindness, goodness, faithfulness, gentleness, and self-control.
—GALATIANS 5:22–23 NLT

Having joy in the work that you do isn't some type of luxury. It is a by-product of being connected to Jesus and putting God's work first. Joy is a sign that God's spirit is working in you and through you. When a statement inspires you to pursue something because you value the intrinsic fulfillment that it provides, a.k.a. joy, then you'll notice a greater interest and persistence to perform your best in all areas of life and ministry.

Whereas, if you are motivated by gaining more money, approval, social standing, or power, then your focus is on the self and your purpose is about getting and being served rather than giving and serving.

Factor Three: The statement should be hopeful and faithful.

Hope that is seen is no hope at all. Who hopes for what they already have? But if we hope for what we do not yet have, we wait for it patiently.

—ROMANS 8:24–25 NIV

Now faith is confidence in what we hope for and assurance about what we do not see... And without faith it is impossible to please God.

—HEBREWS 11:1, 6 NIV

Faith and hope are crucial in our walk with Christ. In these verses, Paul points out that if we are to hope for something, it must be something that we do not yet have and do not yet fully see, which requires faith.

As mentioned earlier in this section, a vision and mission that simply reflects the person we already are or can easily be will lead to a statement that is dull and uninspiring.

A hopeful and faithful statement is one that arouses a feeling of progress, opens possibilities, and inspires us to flourish. A statement that does not evoke this sense of abundance can leave space for one to feel they are working because they are lacking in some area.

When we feel we don't have enough, we tend to rationalize why *we* should have *more*, and *others* should have *less*. When we feel we are deficient, our focus is on the self. Our relationships and how we interact with others become parasitic. Either we take away from others because we feel they have too much, or we feel others are taking away from us because we don't have enough to give out.

When it comes to worry and feeling as though we don't have enough, this is what Jesus has to say:

Do not worry, saying, "What shall we eat?" or "What shall we drink?" or "What shall we wear?" For the pagans run after all these things, and your heavenly Father knows that you need them. But seek first his kingdom and his righteousness, and all these things will be given to you as well.

—MATTHEW 6:31-33 NIV

BONUS DAY 21

Bonus Step 6: It's too dangerous to goal alone

Before we start this bonus section, I want to encourage you to take a moment to celebrate how far you have come. The fact that you're this far along in the journey tells me you are not just a dreamer. You are a doer. You are someone who takes action and steps out in faith.

Since I know you're the type who has put in the best effort, I thought I would give you my best effort by providing you the tools you need to further your growth.

What you get out of this book and these bonus sections, is in exact proportion to the time and effort you put in.

Just how the amount of oil the poor widow could get in 2 Kings 4 was proportional to the amount of jars she came ready with... the amount you get out of this next section will depend on how much you're willing to get out of it.

So continue to go all in and come ready to be filled up!

* * *

Ideally, if life were perfect, we'd be able to live out our vision and mission in every role at every moment. It's easy to stay in harmony with our values when we are feeling good, have a sense of security, and have no struggles. But this isn't realistic, which is why it is important to be prepared.

Jesus talks about the importance of being prepared in Matthew 24:

Keep watch, because you do not know the day on which your Lord will come. But understand this: If the homeowner had known in which watch of the night the thief was coming, he would have kept watch and would not have let his house be broken into. For this reason, you also must be ready, because the Son of Man will come at an hour you do not expect.

—MATTHEW 24:42–44 NIV

Just how we should be prepared for Jesus's return, or a robber in the night, we too should be prepared for when we are tested. The opportunities that bring about fruitfulness and prove whether or not we are living by our values come when we need to resist instant gratification and make some sacrifices.

By having proactive and preventive steps to remain integral, we are essentially preparing for the robber. This preparedness gives us greater control to live out our virtues and see the fruit that is produced from living a life of integrity.

With no vision, no mission, and no plan, our growth, joy, and purpose are dependent on circumstances and other people, which are totally out of our control.

Trying to control every situation and every person to best meet our growth would be like trying to control the weather, the wind, or the waves in the sea. However, despite not being able to control the things around us, we can control how we respond to the things around us and who we put our faith in.

Action: Follow these prompts. Pick a single role and answer all the questions before answering the same questions for the next role.

1. Look at each individual role from your vision and mission. Think to yourself and reflect on the times where you behaved in a way that broke integrity with yourself while in that role.

    A. What factors led to the misbehavior?

    B. How did external factors influence your behavior?

2. What is one thing you could have done prior to the misbehavior in order to have prevented your actions?

3. If a situation arises where you are about to break integrity, what can you do that'll stop, or potentially de-escalate, the feelings to break integrity?

4. What's an action you can do that will prepare and help promote you to positively live out your vision and mission while also avoiding the possibility of breaking integrity?

Chapter 6

WATERING, GROOMING, AND WEEDING

BONUS DAY 22: SUPPORTING AND CATALYZING GROWTH

Since you are at this chapter, you have proven your sincerity to grow and be responsible with more. You've gone above and beyond what most have done.

Only a small percentage of people take the initiative to get a resource that will help to grow them. And an even smaller percentage of people follow through. As we get closer to wrapping up,

I want to say thank you for coming this far. Let us finish strong by going through the tools and tips that will equip you to continue to maintain and further grow the garden you have started.

You might be thinking, "Started my garden? I thought we just finished making the garden after making the vision and mission statements?"

Your garden isn't some statements or the notes you've taken on this journey. Your garden is your life and your ministry. The garden is where you plant your statement.

Just like any garden, you don't just plant and leave. You need to manage the ground and care for the plants that you intend to grow.

Watering, Grooming, and Weeding are proactive actions. To have a beautiful garden, a beautiful home, even something as simple as a clean room or desk requires proactive action. Homes don't randomly form. Messes aren't randomly cleaned. Business plans aren't randomly put together. And a fulfilling life doesn't come without conscious proactive decision-making.

Your first proactive decision was going through this book. The second was participating in the exercises. Now the third will be to follow through on your hard work. This chapter will help ensure that you are able to follow through with maintaining your garden and produce the most fruit from it.

This final section will focus on giving you the tools to do three things:

1. Water your garden (being intentional about growth)

2. Groom your garden (focusing and maximizing the fruitful areas)

3. Manage Weeds and Pests (removing future setbacks and downfalls)

Keep in mind, the information in this last section is going to be packed with applicable information. In fact, the information in this section will be further expanded upon in a future book. To learn more information about future books and additional resources, go to PlantingYourPurpose.com.

You won't be able to apply all the information in this final chapter at once. Therefore, feel free to review this last section for inspiration on how to maintain your newly fruitful garden.

WATERING: BEING INTENTIONAL ABOUT GROWTH

We must not be led to believe that the Disciplines are only for spiritual giants and hence beyond our reach, or only for contemplatives who devote all their time to prayer and meditation. Far from it. God intends the Disciplines of the spiritual life to be for ordinary human beings: people who have jobs, who care for children, who wash dishes and mow lawns. In fact, the Disciplines are best exercised in the midst of our relationships with our husband or wife, our brothers and sisters, our friends and neighbors.

—RICHARD J. FOSTER

Farmers are some of the hardest working and most persistent

people in the world. Back in elementary school, I would visit the farm in our local area called Springdale Farms. I would go there all the time as a kid and hangout with my good friend Alan. We would chase chickens, pick corn, and help on the farm as best as an elementary school kid could. Alan's dad, Mr. Jarvis, owned and ran the farm.

In my eyes, Mr. Jarvis was the physical embodiment of what it meant to be a farmer. His hands were rough, his clothes were plaid, and you could just sense the joy he got from farming radiate from his skin. Rain or shine, Mr. Jarvis was up before the roosters' crowed and would immediately tackle the most important tasks for the day.

There is a lot to do when it comes to managing a farm, and a good farmer will know what to do, when to do it, and how to do it well. One could say that farmers religiously follow a set of practices that help them get the most growth from the seeds they sow.

Farmers understand that the hard work they put in today will lead to a greater harvest tomorrow.

The lazy man will not plow because of winter; He will beg during harvest and have nothing.

—PROVERBS 20:4 NKJV

If we are to be intentional about our growth, we should know how to structure our disciplines so that it can maximize our progress. Doing so will help to reap greater benefits that come from living in our vision and mission.

But don't fall into the trap of thinking that rituals or disciplines are reserved only for the hardworking farmer or the spiritual elite. We are to be intentional about how we are spending our time and investing our energy in everyday life, which includes the mundane moments.

As you read on, try to imagine how you can practically apply these lessons in your everyday interactions and tasks.

Lesson 1: Recognizing the Seasons

There is a time for everything, and a season for every activity under the heavens: a time to be born and a time to die, a time to plant and a time to uproot.

—ECCLESIASTES 3:1-2 NIV

We've already established that farmers are some of the most hardworking people on the planet, but they are also the most strategic. They know they can't be out in the field doing the same work in spring like they can do in winter. When the winter season comes, it demands different tasks to be done.

Plants need to be watered more frequently in the hot summer than they would need in spring. And plants in winter shouldn't be watered because the water can freeze the plant and potentially kill it.

We need to recognize the season of life we are in.

Here are some questions you can reflect on:

- Is the work we are doing trying to compensate for a season that has passed?

- Are we getting the adequate rest we need in order to continue to perform at our fullest?

- Are we resting too much during a season where we should be out in the fields, working our hardest?

Lesson 2: Adapting to the Storms in Life

As Jesus was walking along, he saw a man who had been blind from birth. "Rabbi," his disciples asked him, "why was this man born blind? Was it because of his own sins or his parents' sins?"

"It was not because of his sins or his parents' sins," Jesus answered. "This happened so the power of God could be seen in him."

—JOHN 9:1–3 NLT

Sometimes our struggles can provide opportunities to better recognize God's goodness and power in our life. We may face a storm that we can't get through on our own. It appears the only way we can make it through is with God's help. Fortunately, the journey we are on is one that can only happen with God.

Rituals may help provide an environment that catalyzes growth. But it is God who makes the seed take root. Holding on to rituals as though they will save us is like holding our breath and hoping it will provide enough buoyancy to keep us afloat. During the storms, we are to rely on God in order to remain integral to who God made us to be.

Therefore, during these storms it is best to:

- Be flexible

- Hold true to the values you identified with on this journey

- Always look to God

When we come out of the storm, our endurance will grow and so will our faith in God.

Lesson 3: Sabbath

Then Jesus said to them, "The Sabbath was made to meet the needs of people, and not people to meet the requirements of the Sabbath."

—MARK 2:27 NLT

Take my yoke upon you and learn from me, for I am gentle and humble in heart, and you will find rest for your souls.

—MATTHEW 11:29 NLT

Jesus's way is one that fits us. It is one that keeps us close and intimate with him. It is also one that requires us to be moving at his pace. In our society, rest is seen as weak. Ironically, it is only during our times of rest when we get stronger!

Athletes don't get stronger in the gym. They get weaker.

In the gym is where an athlete shows their strength. But it is outside of the gym when they are recovering that they grow their strength. Therefore, make time to receive the rest Jesus offers.

Lesson 4: When and Where

This step is a little less spiritual and more so just blunt advice. When you are creating rituals or disciplines, you should know when and where you'll do them.

If you can answer *when* you'll do your ritual and *where* you'll do it, you are statistically more likely to follow through in doing said ritual consistently.

Lesson 5: Deeper Renewal

Create in me a pure heart, O God, and renew a steadfast spirit within me. Do not cast me from your presence or take your Holy Spirit from me. Restore to me the joy of your salvation and grant me a willing spirit, to sustain me.

—PSALM 51:10–12 NIV

Often a light sprinkle of water isn't enough to reach the seeds or deeper roots. If the soil that you are watering is hot and dry, light watering can simply evaporate upon contacting the soil or get soaked up so quickly it doesn't penetrate deeply.

Sprinkling water over a vast area of your garden would be like briefly trying to recover yourself physically, emotionally, spiritually, and mentally. Although all the areas may be acknowledged, there is no deep recovery in any of the areas if you breeze over them.

Typically, when we feel drained and are trying to recover, we tend to focus on one preferred area, and end up not fully experiencing recovery in the other areas.

For example, having rituals that just take care of you physically, like exercise, may indirectly help you recover you emotionally, mentally, and spiritually. But the recovery in those other areas is diffused and doesn't create deep rejuvenation.

Another example is reading. It may help you recover mentally and indirectly help you recover physically, emotionally, or spiritually. But again, that recovery is diffused.

So make sure your rituals and disciplines aim to respectively replenish you physically, emotionally, spiritually, and mentally.

Often one ritual can't bring about adequate renewal and nourishment in all areas. Therefore, find ways that can feed you fully in all four areas, while also being aware of activities that may feed one area and drain another.

For example, socializing with friends helps me to recover emotionally. But mentally, I feel tired afterwards. Therefore, I need to balance out how much I socialize so that I won't be too drained mentally, which can start to negatively impact me in other areas.

BONUS DAY 23
GROOMING: SNIPPING BRANCHES

As your garden begins to develop, the various plants that sprout up will begin to grow branches. Branches aren't inherently bad. But if one plant has too many branches, then those very branches will begin taking energy away from the fruits that are meant to grow.

A tomato vine with a lot of branches might be able to produce a lot of tomatoes, but those tomatoes will be small and unable to grow. Since so much energy is being invested in keeping the branches alive, there isn't enough energy and nutrients to sustain making the tomatoes any larger.

But a tomato vine with only a few branches is capable of growing larger and more delicious tomatoes. If the plant is not investing most of its energy in keeping a lot of branches alive, it can focus more energy on the few tomatoes that it does have!

This same thing is true in our lives and in ministry. We may already have some tasks that we need to cut off. Or maybe we are starting to form some new tasks that can produce some fruit. Either way, too many tasks, too much on our schedule, or too much on our mind, isn't good for the health of the individual, the ministry, or the growth of the fruit.

HOW TO PREVENT NEW BRANCHES

One tactic that works best to prevent new unnecessary branches from forming is to get better at saying *no*.

In order to say yes to the important things, we need to get better at saying no to the unimportant things. We can see this in Luke 9:59-62 when the men agree to follow Jesus but first insist that they finish prior tasks:

Jesus said to another man, "Follow me." But he replied, "Lord, first let me go and bury my father."

Jesus said to him, "Let the dead bury their own dead, but you go and proclaim the kingdom of God."

Still another said, "I will follow you, Lord; but first let me go back and say goodbye to my family."

Jesus replied, "No one who puts a hand to the plow and looks back is fit for service in the kingdom of God."

—LUKE 9:59-62 NIV

The tasks that these men had weren't bad. But they were distractions that were keeping them from following Jesus's call. These tasks, opportunities, and obligations demanded time, attention, and resources that would have been more fruitful if they were invested toward Jesus.

Society teaches us to fill in our schedule as much as possible. More work *does not* equate to more fruitfulness. Busyness is most often used to avoid the few important and uncomfortable tasks in our life. We may find ourselves spending all day pulling weeds, waving away pests, and doing numerous other activities. Yet none of them really bring us closer to our goals.

Vilfredo Pareto, an Italian engineer, sociologist, economist, political scientist, and philosopher, came up with something called the 80/20 Principle. He noticed that 80 percent of his garden peas were produced by only 20 percent of the peapods he had planted. That's true for any plant. You don't need to plant ten seeds to get ten seeds back. You can plant one seed and get hundreds of seeds in return.

The same idea is true when we write out our to-do list. What you'll find is that a majority of the results you get come from only a fraction of the tasks we do throughout the day.

You may have tasks that *are* important. But if the task doesn't have you utilizing your strengths, gifts, purpose, or experiences that were discovered throughout this book, then the task *can* and *should* be handled by someone who's strengths, gifts, purpose, and experiences do line up with the task.

In Hebrews, Paul says it like this:

Since we are surrounded by such a huge crowd of witnesses to the life of faith, let us strip off every weight that slows us down, especially the sin that so easily trips us up. And let us run with endurance the race God has set before us.

—HEBREWS 12:1 NLT

If something doesn't bring you closer to your goals or doesn't line up with your vision and mission, then you need to say no. It's easier to say no when you are able to look at the activity in light of where God is leading you. If it doesn't align with the vision or mission, then it's best for someone else to fill the role who is called to do it.

Here are some wonderful statements to try out:

- "I'll have to say no for now. But if things change, can I get back in contact with you later?"

- "Let me get back to you after I check my schedule."

- "Thank you for offering me this opportunity, but since I am working on focusing my ministry down to just the few areas where God is calling me to be, I'll have to say no for now."

If you're like me and say yes to things before you even check your calendar, saying no can be both *really* challenging and make you feel as though you are missing out.

Let me emphasize that it may feel really challenging to say no. It may even feel like I'm asking you to say no to *everything*! But if you are like me and say yes to things frequently or are more inclined to immediately say yes, then people like us have to be more proactive at saying no.

The real goal here isn't to cram more into our day; it's to do less but focus more on the truly important things. It's about focusing on doing the few things that matter most.

You will have to use your own judgment and ask God for some wisdom with making the right judgment.

If you find yourself struggling to start removing tasks, then ask yourself:

- Can this be handled by someone else?

  - If yes, then have the other person do it.

  - If no, then move to the next question.

- Will this task get me closer to achieving my goals?

  - If it won't bring you closer to your goal, then you should try to remove it from your to-do list.

  - If it does bring you closer, then do it.

Before you commit yourself to something you should remember that every time you say *yes* to one thing, you are saying *no* to everything else you can do during that time.

Ask yourself these questions when planning your to-do list:

- What activities take up 20 percent of your resources (time, energy, money, etc.) but yield 80 percent of your desired outcome?

- Now think of the inverse. What 20 percent of the activities in your life are causing 80 percent of your problems and unnecessary stresses?

BONUS DAY 24
WEEDING: REMOVE THE WEEDS IN YOUR LIFE

Weeds are not something we ever try to get. They seem to almost magically appear, requiring no conscious effort.

Just how a garden doesn't *try* and get weeds, as leaders, we don't *try* to schedule unbeneficial tasks in the week. It takes no effort to get junk email, and we don't need to hunt for things that will distract us.

If we aren't intentional about removing the weeds in our life, then those weeds will choke out all the good that might be trying to grow in it.

Some other seed fell among thorny weeds, which grew and choked the good plants... And what is the seed that fell among the thorny weeds? That seed is like the person who hears the teaching but lets worries about this life and the temptation of wealth stop that teaching from growing. So the teaching does not produce fruit in that person's life.

—MATTHEW 13:7, 22 EXB

In this verse, Jesus points out that the weeds that came up to strangle teaching of the kingdom were worry and the desire to have more, which stem from Envy and Greed.

These spiritual weeds can bring about over-commitment of our time, energy, and ability. Worry, envy, and greed can sway good decisions into a whirlwind of different directions that can choke out the truly great things that God wants to grow in our life.

Not managing these spiritual weeds by prayerfully examining and reflecting can create a sense of being overwhelmed and anxious. In extreme cases, the weeds you neglect to manage in your own garden can lead to weeds spreading and growing in the gardens of those around you.

At first, the information you're going to learn may take some time to adopt. Keep in mind, to get more information, additional resources, and videos on the topics discussed in this section, you can find them at PlantingYourPurpose.com. You won't be able to apply it all at once. But after some practice, you'll be able to kill these weeds before they even have a chance to grow.

To better understand how to remove these weeds, we need to first understand each weed.

Worry

Dwelling on worry isn't helpful, healthy, or productive. Rick Warren, pastor of Saddleback Church, says that worry is like being in a rocking chair. You're moving a lot but aren't going anywhere.

When we are concerned with something we *can* act on, then we should act on it. Therefore, worrying about something we can change renders worry useless.

When we are concerned with something we *cannot* act on, then worrying won't prevent or produce a desired outcome. Therefore, worrying about something we have no control over is unproductive.

Jesus has a lot to say on worry in Matthew 6:25–33. It's a great read, and I recommend you take the time to go through it.

If we are worried about something we cannot change, then it requires reflection and moving on.

If we are worried about something we can act on, then it requires action.

You'll find that many worrisome thoughts are imaginary. What I mean is we meditate on these problematic outcomes as opposed to thinking of ways to reduce the chances of that outcome from even occurring. Our minds are simply conjuring up worst-case scenarios.

For example, worrying that no one will come to your small group is a common concern.

If you think no one will come because the time and location weren't clearly communicated, then you can act right now! Contact everyone you invited, clarify the time and location, and don't worry.

If you are worried that no one will come to the group because they don't like the content, then you can act right now! Ask the people in your group what their thoughts are on the topic, get feedback, and adjust where needed.

If you are worried that the time isn't good for everyone, then you can act right now! Adjust the date or time to meet the needs of others.

You see, if the thought is explored more deeply, you may discover that the worrying is coming from something we could handle.

To worry that no one will show up, to worry no one will like the content, and to worry the time isn't good is to worry about something you have no direct control over. When you notice a worry thought, spend time examining it. Explore your thoughts more prayerfully and with curiosity, and then act on them.

Action: Feel free to explore your worrying thoughts by asking yourself two things:

- Am I worried about something that is possible?

- Is there any positive action I can take right now?

If you answer no to either of those questions, then you have a spiritual weed sprouting up. So when you are worried, here are some steps you can take to handle it:

1. Become aware that you are worrying.

2. Shift your focus away from the worrying thought by imagining yourself literally letting it go.

3. Gently and prayerfully feel what God's spirit may be trying to reveal to you.

4. What kind of bodily feeling is the Spirit directing your focus on?

5. Ask God, "What is it that I am really worried about?"

6. Patiently wait for God to respond.

What you are feeling may be emotions that God's spirit is shedding awareness on. Gently and prayerfully lean into this and ask God to reveal to you what you are *really* worried about. Doing this will allow you to attack the weed at the root, which will make it harder for the weed to sprout up again.

Every worrying thought should be examined with the two questions:

1. Is this thought possible?

2. Is there anything I can do to act right now?

Envy

Then I observed that most people are motivated to success because they envy their neighbors. But this, too, is meaningless—like chasing the wind.

—ECCLESIASTES 4:4 NLT

There was a man all alone; he had neither son nor brother. There was no end to his toil, yet his eyes were not content with his wealth. "For whom am I toiling," he asked, "and why am I depriving myself of enjoyment?" This too is meaningless—a miserable business!

—ECCLESIASTES 4:8 NIV

The man in this story kept his focus on accumulating money. Yet he didn't have anyone to leave his property, items, or wealth to. Eventually, he took a moment to step back and reflect on his life, asking "Why am I doing this? Who am I doing this for?" He had given up his life and literally deprived himself of enjoyment, and he didn't know why.

This man was chasing the wind.

"Chasing the wind" is a phrase that is packed with significance. It represents an endless task, one that has no finish line, no clearly defined end, and provides nothing physical or tangible: no peace, no satisfaction, and no contentment.

When we try to pursue things from an envious heart, it is like chasing the wind because it never ends, and we lose true satisfaction in life. It becomes impossible to enjoy our own accomplishments.

Andy Stanley says envy catches people in the "ER" factor. People will always have something that is slightly newER, fastER, slowER, biggER, smallER, loudER, quietER, or trendiER than you.

However, this doesn't mean we shouldn't try to be our best selves or accomplish great things. When we read the rest of the verse that started this section, it says,

"Fools fold their idle hands, leading them to ruin." And yet, "Better to have one handful with quietness than two handfuls with hard work and chasing the wind."

—ECCLESIASTES 4:5-6 NLT

What we learn from this verse is that it is both unwise to do nothing and unwise to seek success out of envy for what others have and where they are in life.

Therefore, instead of trying to have two handfuls of trying to keep up with those around you, it's better to have one handful of being the person you were designed and created to be. When we are truly being ourselves, we may not have bigger, better, newer things than another. But we will have more tranquility, more satisfaction, and greater contentment in our lives, even if we have less.

Not only should we be cautious of comparing our material possessions, but we should guard our hearts against measuring each other's spiritual direction.

If we waste our time measuring the purpose that God has for our life, with the purpose God has for someone else's life, then we will never be satisfied. We'll either be proud and boastful because we are *further* or *better* than someone else. Or we'll be envious because they are *further* or *better* than us.

What is it to us if God is leading someone else down a different path? The thing Jesus says we must do is to follow him (John 21:18–22).

I want to finish this section on envy with this verse:

A heart at peace gives life to the body, but envy rots the bones.

—PROVERBS 14:30 NIV

Peace and envy are like oil and water. They don't mix. You cannot have peace while you are pursuing a vision with envious motivations.

Greed

There's more to life than gaining. Our desire for Jesus's involvement in our life shouldn't be for materialistic motives. The type of riches and relationship God wants for us won't thrive in an environment of greed. A life well lived is not measured or found in the abundance of possessions. We need to be giving. Although we may be wealthy, it doesn't mean our relationship with God is healthy.

Jesus spoke a lot on the topic of money and greed. One of the most perplexing yet enriching lessons on greed that Jesus shares is found in Luke 16:1-9, where he talks about "The Shrewd Manager."

In this parable, Jesus isn't trying to imply that we should use others' money for our own gain. When we analyze the text carefully, we see that Jesus is commemorating the idea that the manager is using his wits to maneuver wealth in order to secure his future.

Jesus says in the passage that *when* money is gone, we want to make sure that we have eternal dwelling. In Jesus, we have secured an eternal future. But when our decisions stem from feelings of joblessness and homelessness in eternity, then our motives are driven by deficiency and scarcity.

Those who are motivated by greed go from using money to help people to using people to make money.

The dishonest manager quickly realizes that his drive to be deceitful to people in order to gain wealth was fruitless.

The manager needed help with joblessness and homelessness. He wanted to secure his career and have a home. Jesus elevated this dishonest manager not to commemorate his dishonesty but to point out the importance of securing our future and the evil that comes from greed.

Action:

- List out the reasons you have used to convince yourself to act greedy in the past.

- How does Jesus combat these excuses in Luke 12:17–34?

WRAP-UP

Live life according to the values Jesus has deeply planted into your heart. You can imagine this vision and mission like a set of glasses. They simply help to focus and fix your sights on the way of Jesus. Allow him to personally transform and make your life, your relationships, and ministry fruitful.

At its core, your vision and mission will always be an expression of your deepest values found in Jesus. When you take the time to review and reflect on it, you are consciously trying to align your beliefs with your behavior.

Ruth Barton, author of *Strengthening the Soul of Your Leadership*, shares a lot of wisdom on the topic of transformation. She says that the process is full of mystery and is outside our ability to accomplish completely on our own. God is the one who initiates and guides the process, ultimately bringing it to fruition.

We should be humbled by this realization as well as relieved not to need to bear such a heavy responsibility to change ourselves or others. We are to faithfully do the one thing we can do, which is make the conditions that create an encounter with God in the places where we may need it the most.

Chapter 7

COMPARING BASELINE MEASUREMENTS

BONUS DAY 25: TRACKING YOUR PROGRESS

Now that you have gotten to the end of this book, let us retake the measurements from the beginning and compare the results!

As a side note, feel free to take this every six months. It can be taken as a way to start off the new year, or taken to see how you're feeling as the year wraps up. It can also be a check-up for you in the middle of the year. Or you can take it more frequently, once every other month if you desire.

The amount of times you go through this self-examination is up to you. Take notice of what has changed and what may have stayed the same. Allow yourself time to pray and reflect on these new findings as you continue to go further in your walk with Jesus.

- In a few words, describe how you are currently doing:

- In what ways have you experienced God lately?

- List what has been life-giving:

- List what has been life-draining:

- What things are presently occupying your mind and heart?

From a scale of 1 to 10, 1 being none and 10 being extremely, fill in what you feel for each question.

How excited are you to get to work each morning?

① ② ③ ④ ⑤ ⑥ ⑦ ⑧ ⑨ ⑩

How much do you enjoy what you do for the sake of doing it rather than for what it can provide you?

① ② ③ ④ ⑤ ⑥ ⑦ ⑧ ⑨ ⑩

How accountable do you hold yourself to a set of deeply held values or virtues?

① ② ③ ④ ⑤ ⑥ ⑦ ⑧ ⑨ ⑩

[Greater than 27 means significant sense of purpose]

[Less than 22 means you're going through the motion]

Which areas of your life would like to more fully live out your deeply held values and virtues?

HEALTH

HOME

MINISTRY

WORK

RELATIONSHIPS

SPIRITUALITY

PERSONAL GROWTH

What are some hopes and desires you want to bring to God?

Using the diagram below, reflect on how fulfilled you feel in each area. Put a dot in each section of the diagram. The center represents 0 percent fulfillment. The edge represents 100 percent fulfillment.

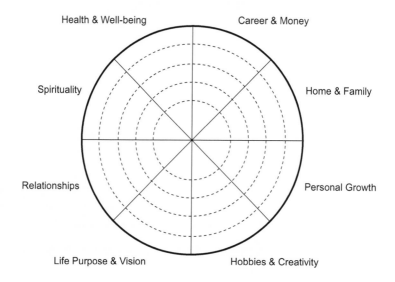

Health & Well-being

Career & Money

Spirituality

Home & Family

Relationships

Personal Growth

Life Purpose & Vision

Hobbies & Creativity

Connect each dot to create a shape on the diagram. As you look at the shape, what are your thoughts or insights?

Write today's date:

ADDED BONUS SECTION

INTEGRITY AND PURPOSE

Bad things do happen; how I respond to them defines my character and the quality of my life. I can choose to sit in perpetual sadness, immortalized by the gravity of my loss, or I can choose to rise from the pain and treasure the most precious gift I have—life itself.

—WALTER ANDERSON

"Integrity" is a word that can be interpreted in many ways, depending on the context in which it is used.

When people talk about the integrity of a house, they are referring to the house's ability to remain whole and intact without falling apart under pressure. When integrity is talked about in a church or political setting, it is often referring to a person's ability to be morally upright and uncompromising.

When I talk about integrity, I'm not referring to morals or ethics, I am referring to the wholeness and internal consistency in one's life. Integrity is made up of unity, completeness, and internal consistency. In the Christians' life, it is expressed by behaving and living according to the values that Jesus teaches. Not living by these values *will* create division, dishonesty, fragility, and disease within you.

"Disease" is defined as being "an abnormality of the structure or function of an organism." This abnormality leads to the life and well-being of the living organism to be negatively affected, most often resulting in death. In fact, disease is the number one killer for all human beings. Heart disease (640,000) alone kills more people yearly than car accidents (36,000), work injuries (5,000), medical malpractice (250,000), firearm deaths (14,000, excluding suicide), and homicide (19,000)[5] combined.

5   Kenneth D. Kochanek, Sherry L. Murphy, Jiaquan Xu, and Elizabeth Arias. "Deaths: Final Data for 2017." *National Vital Statistics Reports* 68, no. 9 (June 24, 2019). https://www.cdc.gov/nchs/data/nvsr/nvsr68/nvsr68_09-508.pdf; Richard Retting and Sam Schwartz Consulting. "Pedestrian Traffic Fatalities by State." Edited by Russ Martin and Kara Macek. Governors Highway Safety Association, February 2019. https://www.ghsa.org/sites/default/files/2019-02/FINAL_Pedestrians19.pdf; US Bureau of Labor Statistics, "Census of Fatal Occupational Injuries Summary, 2018," US Bureau of Labor Statistics, December 17, 2019. https://www.bls.gov/news.release/cfoi.nr0.htm; Michael Daniel. "Study Suggests Medical Errors Now Third Leading Cause of Death in the U.S." Johns Hopkins Medicine, May 3, 2016. https://www.hopkinsmedicine.org/news/media/releases/study_suggests_medical_errors_now_third_leading_cause_of_death_in_the_us; Jennifer Mascia. "Gun Deaths Dropped in 2018, Excluding Suicides." *The Trace*, January 7, 2019. https://www.thetrace.org/2019/01/gun-deaths-2018-america-mass-shootings-suicide/; Kenneth D. Kochanek, Sherry L. Murphy, Jiaquan Xu, and Elizabeth Arias. "Deaths: Final Data for 2017." *National Vital Statistics Reports* 68, no. 9 (June 24, 2019). https://www.cdc.gov/nchs/data/nvsr/nvsr68/nvsr68_09-508.pdf.

Disease: The #1 Killer

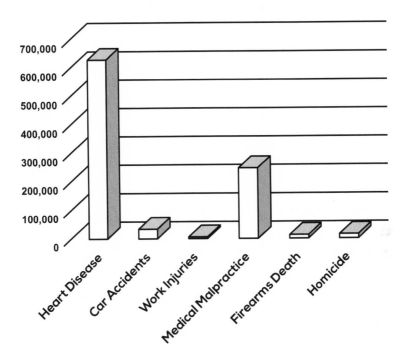

What's fascinating is that disease causes death because the organs, tissues, or cells are behaving dishonestly to the way they were designed.

Which means that the top causes of death are due to *internal* structures being out of alignment, not harmful *external* forces.

Deaths by homicide, car accidents, work injuries, medical malpractice, and firearms are all external forces acting on the individual. But diseases that lead to death are due to internal systems being out of integrity.

When someone has a disease, something within them isn't functioning the way it was intended or designed.

Cells behave certain ways based on how its internal programming responds to external stimuli. Depending on the type of stimuli, the way the cell functions will differ based on how the script, the DNA, inside the cell responds to that stimuli. If the DNA is altered, the way in which the cell responds is also altered.

Imagine a cell is not reproducing how it's supposed to. If its DNA is not telling the cell to replicate enough, you get a greater number of cell deaths as opposed to cell growth, a.k.a. decay. Or let's say the internal script is wrong and an excessive amount of cell growth occurs. This is how cancer forms.

A cell reproducing too much or not enough are both signs of disease. The death and destruction that arise as a result of the disease are all due to the abnormality of the structure or function within the cell.

Essentially, a diseased cell is a cell that does not have integrity.

Cells are programmed to *react* to their environment. Fortunately, we are not bound to behave according to the circumstances and triggers around us. We are capable of consciously making the choice to *act* instead of *react*.

We may not act perfectly all the time. But we should know who we're striving to be, where we're being led, and where we are currently at in our journey.

Self-awareness is a crucial part of having integrity.

The worst thing you can do is lie to yourself by ignoring where you are in life. One cannot become whole if they are not aware of the holes or misalignments in them. That's what the "Cultivating" and "Digging" chapters were all about. Remember that the reason why patients with diabetes didn't seek treatment for infections in limbs such as their feet was because they didn't realize that their feet were infected.

If we are to try and walk with Jesus and be in harmony with Jesus, we need to be conscious of the pace at which we are going through life. If we're not in harmony or on track, we are creating dis-ease within ourselves and our relationship with Jesus. The best thing we can do if we are not in harmony is to look to Jesus and his calling in our lives.

The analogy of Jesus's yoke is packed with wisdom and information on how Jesus wants to guide our lives. This yoke that Jesus offers is the calling and purpose in our life. When a yoke is used for cattle, it is both a means to guide the cattle and to lessen the load that the cattle have to carry.

This is what Jesus offers when he tells us to take the yoke from him. He wants us to be guided by him, be in harmony with him, and be open to allowing him to help carry the burden of life:

Come to me, all you who are weary and burdened, and I will give you rest. Take my yoke upon you and learn from me, for I am gentle and humble in heart, and you will find rest for your souls. For my yoke is easy and my burden is light.

—MATTHEW 11:28–30 NIV

Action: Ask yourself these three questions as a regular checkup to ensure you are growing in integrity:

- What are your values and virtues?

- How have you been living by those values?

- Where have you failed to live by those values and virtues in the past?

WRAP-UP

Living and behaving based on vision and mission doesn't necessarily mean you'll burst into immediate success or transformation. However, values do provide inspiration and guidance for the long term.

Vision and mission will have you approach your various roles in life with purpose and a clearer sense of direction. With clear purpose and direction come greater discernment, greater leadership, and a greater impact. Instead of reacting based on how you feel in the moment, challenges turn into opportunities to respond based on who God is making you to be.

Living in your vision and mission might feel awkward or difficult at first. Don't worry, it's supposed to. Just like driving a car for the first time, you may feel like there are a lot of moving parts and a lot to pay attention to. Ideally, you'll want to get to the point where you are paying sharp but relaxed attention to what you're doing and feeling. You'll also develop a better awareness as to what is going on around you and in you that may influence your feelings and actions.

In the beginning, it'll take a lot of conscious effort. But with persistence, over time, you'll become a natural.

Don't think of your statement as a strict GPS, where you must scrutinize every left and right turn. Your vision and mission are more like a compass instead of a GPS. The compass will always point you north toward your destination. The more north you go, the closer you'll get to the destination and the more accurate and precise your steps will become.

Keep in mind, it's not always easy. There are times when we must endure difficulties. Hard bosses, stressful work environments, even tight finances. Still, when we are guided by clear values, we can choose how to behave from a position of confidence, strength, and self-respect rather than from anger, bitterness, and self-doubt.

Joseph could have been bitter toward his brothers for selling him into slavery and trying to kill him. David could have been angry at King Saul for trying to kill him. But both David and Joseph stayed true to who God had made them to be during those troubling moments.

Even Jesus, who at the time was being murdered, demonstrated God's love by asking God to forgive the very people who were killing him, which ironically were also the very people he came to help.

Jesus could have easily condemned them, rebuked them, or even ended their lives in that moment. Choosing to live with integrity and staying true to the vision and mission may not be the most comfortable or easy option. However, it's not about picking the easy choice, it is about making the right choice.

ENDING THOUGHTS

I want to start this ending thought by emphasizing the importance of knowing who you are in Jesus, knowing who Jesus is, and knowing to follow only Jesus.

In Matthew 4:1-11 and Luke 4:1-13, after Jesus had fasted for forty days, the devil tries to manipulate Jesus. He does this by questioning Jesus's character (Matt 4:3, Luke 4:3), questioning God's character (Matt 4:6, Luke 4:9), and bribing Jesus to turn away from God (Matt 4:9, Luke 4:6-7).

Jesus is able to resist the devil because he knows who provided, he knows who is in control, and he knows who God is.

If Satan's best tactics on Jesus were to question his character, God's character, and God's authority, then we too should be equipped to combat against these same attacks. Therefore, review the lessons and notes from this journey, as they can provide you with the weapons and defenses needed to guard and attack these tactics from the enemy.

Don't forget, the knowledge and tools in this book are more than just offensive and defensive strategies. They are also catalysts for spiritual maturity and development!

As your garden grows, it'll allow for others to be part of what God is growing in your life. Ultimately you want to have your garden, as well as your vision and mission, become so expansive and fruitful that it will help enhance the lives of others around you.

You can probably imagine that a larger garden means more to manage and more to care for. This book can't give all the necessary knowledge to continue to scale the growth you'll initially have. However, you can expect future books to accompany you on your journey as you develop in your walk with Jesus.

Just to clarify, this book won't solve all of one's life or ministry problems indefinitely. As you progress on this journey, you will face new problems. But they will be problems that can lead to more maturity, love, and integrity.

Unfortunately, there are working Christians who are facing unnecessary struggles and discontentment. During the research that was conducted in the making of this book, I realized that a lot of the dissatisfaction and unfulfillment people found in work and in life comes from the inconsistent thoughts and attitudes used for navigating through life.

Many want fulfillment and to live by God's will. However, many make decisions in favor of job security and financial stability while avoiding decisions that may be in favor of God's calling.

I began to see that the things people desire are taking more priority than the God who can provide them. What's wrong is that more people are trying to grow the fruits, the by-products of a good life, without examining the roots, one's relationship and walk with Jesus.

According to Barna Research, 59 percent of millennials and 65 percent of Gen Z want financial independence more than they want to follow their dreams or mature more spiritually.[6] In their research, Barna Research found the ranking of priorities for Gen Z and millennials to be as follows:

Gen Z:
Finish education
Start career
Become financially independent
Follow one's dreams
Enjoy life before having the responsibilities of being an adult
Find out who oneself really is
Travel to other countries
Get married
Become more mature spiritually

Millennials:
Become financially independent
Finish education

---

6   Barna Research, "What Will It Take to Disciple the Next Generation?" Barna Research, August 27, 2019. https://www.barna.com/research/disciple-next-generation/.

Start a career
Find out who oneself really is
Follow one's dreams
Become mature spiritually

It's been said, "If God didn't allow people to eat until they understood their calling, there would be a drastic increase in people finding that calling."

Sadly, the hunger pangs of a deprived spirit aren't noticed as quickly as the discomfort of an empty stomach.

Believing that money and security in material things can provide contentment in life creates major cognitive and spiritual dissonance in the working Christian. The reality is that true peace, fulfillment, and contentment come from following Jesus. A person cannot follow both money and Jesus because they will find themselves loving one and not the other.

The fruitfulness and fulfillment that come from walking with Jesus promote every other area in life, benefiting education, career, finances, relationships, adventure, and one's fulfillment!

Fulfillment comes from following God's will and direction, which means making decisions that can put one's career or finances at risk.

To seek a secure job and financial security first means that God's direction and purpose is put last.

Even when the individual starts to gain financial security, there is a point when more money stops satisfying the life and spirit of the individual. Once the need for things like shelter and food are met, the person is left with a neglected, depressed, and malnourished spirit. The person now finds that they are merely existing inside a life that is empty. The individual can try to feed the spirit with more material things, but it will ultimately not satisfy.

The one that can bring new and refreshing life into a person's spirit is Jesus. Sometimes this is achieved by reexpressing one's faith in him. It may start with confession of the heart or sharing one's mistakes with a trusted church family member. Either way, following Jesus is shown by living like you have a father in heaven and a motive for living.

Step into opportunities where your heart feels God's presence and where you're willing to let God move you. Whether God has you starting in one direction, then quickly pivots you another way, if you surrender your next move to God, and your heart sincerely trusts God on the journey, then I promise you, He will fill you up and show you your purpose.

It all starts with following Him.

Thank you so much for using this guide while on your walk with Jesus. It was a pleasure to write this for you, and I look forward to seeing what good things God produces in you.

If you found that this book was helpful and think it can help someone else in ministry, feel free to contact me by going to PlantingYourPurpose.com, and I will be sure to send you resources and discounts to pass along to those you know.

20% Off
PLANTING YOUR
PURPOSE

VISIT

www.PlantingYourPurpose.com

BONUS
RESOURCES

SCAN ME

ACKNOWLEDGMENTS

I would like to thank everyone in this list. Each of you has contributed in developing me, guiding me, and assisting me in life. Either through helping to produce this book, helping me in my walk with Christ, or developing me as a man. I wouldn't be who or where I am today if it weren't for you all.

(This list is written in alphabetical order.)

Aconda Williams, Amy Ross, Andy Race, Andy Stanley, Annemarie Wörtz, Barb Brinkerhoff, Bedros Keuilian, Ben Taylor, Billy Graham, Carole Kassan, Chris Hones, Craig Groeschel, Cristina Ricci, Dale Carnegie, Dan Kennedy, Dave Falcone, David Martin, David Sayre, Dean Graziosi, Denis Till, Donald Miller, Erica Hoffman, Erin Miller, Fenel Bruna, Gary Dawkins, Gay Hendricks, Golan Kashani, Heather Mandala, Horst Schultz, James Yu, JC Smith, Jeff Bills, Jel Johnson, Jeremy Schep, Jim Collins, Jim Loeher, John Elmer, John Wimber, Josh Race, Lawrence Kassan, Luke Kassan, Mark Tindall, N. T. Wright, Najeeb Jones, Napoleon Hill, Nir Eyl, Pete Wong, Phil McKnight, Randy Petersen, Richard J. Foster, Rick Warren, Ruth Barton, Simon Sinek, Stephen R. Covey, Tiffany Fletcher, Tim Ferriss, Tony Schwartz, Zach Obront.

ABOUT THE AUTHOR

Creator and host of the YouTube channel The Current Christian, **ALEC KASSAN** expresses a clear passion and drive to help others succeed in their walk with Christ and is understood to be a modern-day man after God's heart.

Alec's ingenious outside the box thinking and problem-solving capabilities pairs beautifully with his organized and thorough process of teaching. This combination makes for a refreshing and encouraging way of understanding how to live a fruitful life and what it means to have Jesus at the center of it.

With a Bachelor of Science degree from the School of Education at Syracuse University, Alec brings a unique analytical, yet still imaginative, perspective to the Christian community.